100 Ideas for Secondary Teachers

Gifted and Talented

John Senior

BLOOMSBURY

Other titles in the 100 Ideas for Secondary Teachers series:

100 Ideas for Secondary Teachers: Outstanding Lessons
by Ross Morrison McGill

100 Ideas for Secondary Teachers: Managing Behaviour
by Johnnie Young

Other Secondary titles available from Bloomsbury Education:

100+ Ideas for Supporting Children with Dyslexia by Gavin Reid
and Shannon Green

How to Survive your First Year in Teaching by Sue Cowley

Teacher: Mastering the Art and Craft of Teaching by Tom Bennett

*Why Are You Shouting At Us? The Dos and Don'ts of Behaviour
Management* by Phil Beadle and John Murphy

Contents

Acknowledgements

This book is dedicated to my guide and friend Belle Wallace.

My sincere thanks to Holly Gardner, the book's champion and mentor for her thoughtful, meticulous and determined editing, suggestions, ideas, enthusiasm and patience.

My thanks, also, of course, to Bloomsbury for commissioning and publishing this book.

Introduction

Thank you for picking this book up and opening it with an intention to read it. Read on.

The importance of teaching and learning with gifted and talented students cannot be underestimated. It is the right of students to be supported and educated to the very best of their ability.

Whether you have been teaching ten minutes, ten months or ten years, once you work with students who are more able and talented than you are, you will connect with an attitude that learning is living and nothing else will do.

You, like me, do not need to know all the answers, or the right questions. We just need to be good teachers, which means facilitating learning. It's simple, not tricky.

There are those who see teaching and supporting the gifted and talented cohort as an elitist activity. With all humbleness I suggest to you that these people just don't understand how extremely difficult it can be to be very, very clever.

For the clever child there can be social loneliness as well as intellectual loneliness. For the clever child there may be bullying and challenges resulting from being perceptive that will cause pain, emotional and physical. They need our support and our experience, understanding and readiness to help them achieve in their own way. We need their perceptions, innovations and talents for our own world to develop and mature. We have the privilege of helping them learn to steer through life and whenever we are needed, help them learn to learn.

I know from experience that your students will enjoy the activities and ideas in this book and, if you have made it this far, so will you. Have fun helping students fly. Have fun being a co-learner as well as a teacher. Be a guide, a facilitator and a vital listener.

Finally, let your students work as hard as you do and everyone can go home singing their own song at the end of the day.

John Senior

How to use this book

This book includes quick, easy-to-implement, practical ideas and activities for you to dip in and out of and use to support the gifted and talented students in the secondary classroom.

Each idea includes:

- A catchy title, easy to refer to and share with your colleagues.
- A quote from a teacher or student describing their experiences of the idea.
- A summary of the idea in bold, making it easy to flick through the book and identify an idea you want to use at a glance.
- A step-by-step guide to implementing the idea.

Each idea also includes one or more of the features below.

Teaching tip	Taking it further	Bonus idea ★
Some extra advice on how or how not to run the activity or put the strategy into practice.	Ideas and advice for how to extend the idea or develop it further.	There are 17 bonus ideas in this book that are extra exciting and extra original.

How to use the ideas presented in this book will best be decided by your professional judgement, understanding of the needs and interests of your students and available resources. Start gently if you are new to providing enrichment and extension materials. This book can be used by the new teacher looking for enrichment ideas to use in the classroom right through to the experienced gifted and talented coordinator implementing a whole-school gifted and talented provision. Choose the ideas you find interesting and have a knowledge and understanding of and adapt them to your job role.

The enrichment ideas are designed for secondary-aged students and can be used in their entirety or selected aspects of the ideas can be used. The ideas can also be used within classroom provision as tasks for all, measuring success through differentiated outcomes, or they can be used as stand-alone extra enrichment activities on enrichment days or at your gifted and talented club. Many of the enrichment ideas could be used with an appropriately able student as long-term projects. What I hope most of all is that you will enjoy the ideas and thinking behind them sufficiently to feel you want to produce your own materials. Providing for the gifted and talented should be an enjoyable activity for everyone involved and that includes you!

One word of advice if and hopefully when you do decide to run a club for your gifted and talented cohort, do think carefully about what you call your club: 'The brainy, cleverer than you will ever be gifted and talented club' for example would not be a good idea. There is still a battle for people to accept that the gifted and the talented do need special help and have every right to expect extra assistance as any pupil with a special need. I would suggest, 'The Tuesday club', (very appealing to the humour of your gifted and talented students if in fact you all meet on a Friday) or 'The study group' might be suitably discrete. On the other hand if everyone is comfortable with recognising the gifted and talented then the sky is the limit. Whatever you decide pause to think how it sounds to other ears and what message you are sending to colleagues and other students.

The book is split into ten parts. Every other part provides a collection of original and creative enrichment activities of varying levels. Interspersed between each of these, are the following five sections:

Part 1: Things you need to know: helpful tips and suggestions to help you establish a sound foundation for your ongoing work with the gifted and talented students.

Part 3: Bespoke teaching: this section looks at the range of special needs and considerations to be addressed when working with a broad range of gifted and talented students.

Part 5: Gifted and talented toolbox: ideas and suggestions for areas to concentrate on to develop the personalisation of teaching gifted and talented students.

Part 7: Embedding the provision: ideas and guidance to help establish gifted and talented provision throughout your school and in the classroom.

Part 9: Taking stock and taking control of the gifted and talented provision: ideas to build on your early work and experiences of developing gifted and talented provision. These ideas and activities demonstrate confidence and mastery of your role as a person with responsibility for gifted and talented provision in your school.

However you choose to use these ideas and wherever you deliver them – I hope you enjoy them and enjoy the challenges they present.

Share how you use these ideas in the classroom and find out what other teachers have done using **#100ideas.**

Things you need to know

Part 1

Don't panic!

"I always take a moment to take a calming breath and then I'm 'on stage'."

If and when you start to panic about a lesson or a conversation with students, be ready to call to mind 'instant calm'. Usually instant calm can be achieved by thinking of something, somewhere or someone you feel complete confidence in.

It may be your first teaching responsibility or you may have had many roles in teaching and have a rich experience of classroom practice to call upon. In either case, teaching the gifted and talented for the first time can be something of a shock, though a delightful shock in most cases.

If you do feel nervous or panicked, instant calm is achieved by pausing what you are doing, taking a deep breath and allowing yourself to remember that you are in control of your actions and your task management patterns. For a moment focus on a memory of a still-point; a place you felt peaceful in or a friend with whom you have laughed or just been with, happy in the pleasure and kindness of their company. You only need to remember a calm, happy moment to re-energise yourself, focus and achieve what you want to achieve. Expand the remembered calm and pleasure of calm to enable you to become confident again and easily capable of managing your present challenges.

Remember, one thing at a time! The expectations of senior management, colleagues, parents and carers (not necessarily in that order!) are all manageable if your relationships with your able students are built on a base of secure confidence.

What does it mean?

"The gifted and talented student offers a reflection about learning that is sharper, brighter and more penetrating than most students. I realised early on that teaching the gifted student should be understood as co-learning within a flexible partnership."

Knowing your feelings about giftedness and what it means is important to ensure a professional teacher/co-learner approach.

The most generally accepted description of the term 'gifted and talented' describes the 'gifted' as those with the potential to succeed academically. The 'talented' are seen as those with the potential to be outstanding in the areas of art and design, music, drama and sport.

To be gifted does not of course exclude being talented or vice versa. Defining a human in any way at all with regard to high ability is very difficult and remains a matter of great debate.

Without conducting a major research project, consult with some colleagues and friends, asking them what they think defines or describes a gifted and talented child. Then ask a group of students what they think defines a gifted and talented learner and finally ask a group of identified gifted and talented students how they would define 'highly able'. The differences in views will be as interesting as the agreements about what is perceived as gifted or talented behaviours.

Teaching tip

Many people have deeply held feelings about clever students. These feelings are not always positive and sometimes create conflict between teachers and students. Always be aware that gifted and talented is not a neat and tidy area. Always consider how colleagues who have a negative view of the gifted and talented cohort can be supported to see and appreciate the viewpoint of the gifted and talented student.

Identification

"It's the twinkle in the eye I look for."

Always trust your own feelings and teacher instinct when it comes to identifying an able, gifted and talented child.

Teaching tip

See if you can compile a list of all the posts of responsibility within the school (school prefects, monitors, sports captains), anything that shows a degree of social commitment beyond the norm. Compare the list of opportunities for students to participate in school life with your gifted and talented register. Are there any new positions of responsibility – for example student listener or advocate – that could be created to benefit the school that would allow for the gifted and talented student to rehearse and develop their particular skills and abilities? There are many forms of gifted and talented categories, such as emotional intelligence, that often are not reflected in the core curriculum.

No single method of identification should be relied upon when it comes to identifying a gifted and talented student. It is good practice to use a combination of methods. Wherever available, prior attainment records can be a good starting point, as can the following:

- Self-identification.
- Scores from verbal and non-verbal reasoning tests.
- Checklists (see the one in Idea 5).
- See how different students approach your enrichment activities; identification through differentiated provision can be fun.
- Sometimes a parent or carer provides evidence to support their prediction that their child is exceptional.
- Teacher nomination: ask your colleagues to name who they think are gifted and talented students, off the top of their heads.
- Peer nominations: ask students who is the cleverest at maths, science, negotiation skills or anything at all – students just know. Additionally, ask your gifted and talented group if there is anyone who should also be in the group but isn't. You may be surprised at who they tell you about.
- Success in a formal test: it may be that a student is deliberately identification avoidant, however they usually give themselves away by success in an area that is very important to them.

Stay professional

"I'm not special, just clever."

Gifted and talented students do not necessarily want you to be their friend; they do however, need champions, supporters and facilitators.

Some teachers and administrators in education do not care for gifted and talented students. Some teachers feel threatened by students who they see as challenging their power, control and autonomy. As much as you like the gifted and talented student (you must do, you've read this far!) there will always be students that you do not particularly like or enjoy the company of. This is just the way it goes with people.

The important position to maintain at all times is a professional one. You may feel threatened by the ability of students you teach but you have no need to be. You need to remain organised, be committed to the highest professional standards and be willing to develop as a teacher. Teaching is about forming relationships and not friendships. In your professional life there should be no favourites and no demons. Students will look to you as the arbitrator of equity and fairness so ensure you live up to this role.

Taking it further

Some teachers deny the idea of gifted, able or talented students; they see the labels as divisive. This is a strange position to take when the duty and responsibility of a teacher is to support a learner to achieve the best levels of achievement and self-development possible. Encourage your colleagues to stay professional and develop a rich understanding of the issues connected with giftedness. Find a space in the staff room to display monthly information about pupil achievement; famous quotes about intelligence; good practice statements; different methodologies for teaching and assessing; news cuttings you think are interesting and anything that raises the profile of gifted and talented teaching and students.

Checklists

"I just love questions."

Checklists are a great method for identifying gifted and talented children.

Work through the checklist below. Does this list, or part of this list bring any of your students to mind?

- thinks quickly with unusual accuracy
- enjoys puns and word play
- can work in a systematic manner
- demonstrates extended interest and focus on a task
- can apply skills from different areas to resolve a problem
- can apply knowledge to novel situations
- can communicate ideas and thoughts well
- will apply themselves to a task in a sustained way
- can express themselves in a creative way
- demonstrates unusual empathy for others
- possesses a particular dexterity or physical ability/skill
- can make informed and assured judgements
- is quick to master new ideas and information
- demonstrates great passion for an area
- uses a wide vocabulary with high levels of fluency and originality
- sometimes leaps to solutions without appearing to require intermediate actions
- enjoys playing with ideas and data
- demonstrates a creative and productive mind.

Teaching tip

Not all gifted and talented children will tick all of the boxes in this checklist but will tick just enough of them to raise your suspicions of their abilities. Ensure you use a variety of identification methods alongside the checklist method when identifying gifted and talented students, as different children will shine in different areas and ways.

Taking it further

Invite your students to complete the checklist and see how they mark themselves and evidence their choices. What do they think of the checklist? Is there anything they think is missing? Invite them to produce an improved checklist for future use by you and your colleagues.

Managing parents

"Why isn't my child in the gifted and talented group?!"

Ensure your school has clear and unambiguous policies for the identification and provision of gifted and talented students that meet the needs of all children in the school; then make sure you are very familiar with them and can clearly explain them to parents.

Most parents consider their children to be clever and many like to make their views clear to the school. There is often a status attached to having a child assigned the gifted and talented label. Be familiar with all the activities, clubs and opportunities that are available throughout your school and where appropriate, the wider educational environment. Be ready to explain to parents that careful identification processes are followed to ensure that children participate in activities that are appropriate to their skills and, importantly, suited to their individual happiness and sense of achievement. A school should offer opportunities for a student to enrich and deepen their own particular interests and not necessarily those of their parents.

There is no easy answer to a parent who feels their child should be in the gifted and talented group even when it is clear that it is the last thing the particular student wants or needs. You will need to show parents the school policy, how the policy is implemented and what is available to extend and enrich the school life of that parent's son or daughter through other activities that the school offers. Make the policy and the strategy for implementing the policy completely transparent. Much can be learnt from the school 's special educational needs coordinator (SENCO) as to the best way to work with parents with issues that can be highly emotional.

Teaching tip
Never succumb to parent pressure that occasionally can be about seeing the clever child as a 'social trophy'. Always listen and consider the views of parents, as they do know their children in a different way to you, but do not act without evidence to support your actions. Remember, you have the data, the experience of colleagues and your own experience to help you make decisions.

The learning contract

"Our teacher is always angry on Friday morning because she goes out with her boyfriend on Thursday night. We just keep quiet."

You are a role model. The gifted and talented student will learn from you as he or she moves towards adulthood.

Gifted and talented students need you to show your professionalism and duty of care to them through consistency and attention to them as people who are three-dimensional and not just as 'Sheila or Danny who is good at maths'. They hope you will not patronise them. They will, of course, expect you to be busy with everyone else but also they expect that you will find time for them. In other words, they expect for you to keep your side of the learning contract.

Monitor yourself. If you say you want homework handed in on a certain day and time, stick with this decision. If homework is expected to be returned to students at a certain time then make sure it is. If you can't manage to do this why should your students? The learning contract between teacher and student is of exceptional importance to the gifted and talented student. If you are encountering difficulties when managing your workload then seek out a colleague you trust or who seems to be a wonder teacher and ask them how they manage their workload.

Bonus idea ★

It would be a brave teacher who would ask their gifted and talented group to rate their performance in meeting their needs. Their views, however, will improve your teaching effectiveness so I highly recommend it! Students usually speak their mind freely when they trust the people involved, keep your end of the learning contract and build up your trust to gain honest, invaluable feedback.

Identifying low self-esteem

"Annie introduced herself on the first night of a residential course for gifted children by saying 'I don't know why my school sent me. I'm not clever'."

Never praise for the sake of praising; the gifted and talented student will see right through it.

Low self-esteem may be brought about by many different influences such as genetic factors, physical appearance, socioeconomic status, peer pressure, bullying and additionally, in the case of the gifted and talented student, a sense of intellectual worthlessness and severe emotional isolation which can be devastating for a bright individual.

Individuals with low self-esteem can be very critical of themselves and depend on the approval of others for their own evaluation of self-worth. Low self-esteem management is an extremely complex challenge. There is never one single cause and it often shows itself in a combination of the following ways:

- heavy self-criticism and dissatisfaction
- hypersensitivity to criticism and a well-developed skill set regarding defensive behaviour
- an inability to make decisions
- an exaggerated fear of mistakes
- an overwhelming need to please
- a desperate unwillingness to displease
- seeking perfection when perfection is not achievable
- exaggerated sense of guilt
- a negative outlook regarding all aspects of the student's life.

Teaching tip

The student with low self-esteem will be likely to believe that a person's approval of them is dependent on their performance, both academic and social. It is not easy to reach through this barrier. A consistent approach to meaningful praise and encouragement is required by you, the significant other.

Intelligence tests

"Is this the right question?"

Intelligence tests are another way of identifying your academically gifted and talented students.

Intelligence tests are used to give an overview of an individual's cognitive processes concerning areas such as comprehension, reasoning and the ability to recall information. As we know in education the use of standardised tests aims to produce a numerical standard and comparator for students.

The two most widely known and used standardised intelligence tests are the Stanford-Binet Intelligence Scale and the Wechsler Intelligence Scales. The Stanford-Binet Intelligence Scale measures intelligence across four areas as well as giving an overall score for cognitive potential. The four areas are:

- verbal reasoning
- abstract/visual reasoning
- quantitative reasoning
- short-term memory.

Wechsler believed intelligence to be an aspect of personality and not an isolated quality and his thinking was concerned with testing the capacities of acting purposefully, thinking rationally and dealing effectively with the environment. The Wechsler Intelligence Scales now used consist of tests to evaluate reasoning and intellectual attitudes.

Not all gifted and talented children will necessarily do well when completing intelligence tests. The more able the student, the more possibilities there are for creativity and therefore a variety of potential answers to be generated.

Look after yourself

"I find screaming helps calm me down. Not in front of my class though!"

However anxious you may feel about working with students who are potentially more able than you are, stay focused on your skills and experience as a teacher and make sure you are managing your workload efficiently.

Working with very able people is not about competing with them, controlling them, belittling them or abusing them. Working with gifted and talented students is about helping people to achieve their full potential. It is a privilege to help students grow. Support them when the pressures and demands of their lives combine to overwhelm them.

If you are finding it difficult to manage your role and the experience of working with gifted and talented students, be careful to look at all the pressures that may be bearing down on you. You may actually be anxious and worried because you are doing too much, expecting unrealistic achievements of yourself, lacking in exercise and sleep. Take time to look at your working day and week as well as looking at what you do or don't do out of work. Your anxieties about working with gifted and talented children may actually be misplaced worries that can be solved by asking your self the following questions and making changes:

- Do you make time each day for relaxation and fun?
- Are you getting the emotional and professional support you need?
- Are you taking care of your mind and body?
- Are you overloaded with responsibilities?
- Are people taking advantage of you?
- Do you ask for help when you need it?

Teaching tip

If you're feeling isolated or unsupported, find someone you trust to confide in. Talk to someone, you are not a burden to their ears, most people want to listen and having someone listen to you does help you see the issues more clearly. Just talking about your worries can make them seem less frightening.

Encrichment ideas 1

Part 2

206 bones

"I wish I had wings."

It is always interesting to have an idea to discuss with gifted and talented students that has no right answer and involves thinking about oneself.

There are 206 bones in the adult human body. Ask your students two questions:

1 What would you consider the minimum number of bones required for a human body to function in normal circumstances?
2 Would additional bones be helpful in the future? Where would any new bones be placed?

Ask students to produce a cardboard skeleton showing where the new bones would be located and how they would function. The new skeletons can then be compared with normal skeletons and an exhibition could be arranged.

It is also interesting to discuss a new sense, skill or ability within the concept of super heroes. Why do these archetypes persist?

For information, the femur is the longest bone in the human body and is located in the thigh. In adults, it can reach a length of over 19 inches (0.5 m). The smallest bone in the human body is the stirrup bone, the stapes, one of three bones that make up the middle ear.

Taking it further

Ask students to consider the bone arrangement in birds and to research the weight/lift ratio of weight to wingspan. They could then estimate the number and size of bones that would be needed if a human being had wings. It would be fascinating to compare their research conclusions with the representation of angels in religious paintings.

Bonus idea ★

Weight is the measure of force on an object due to gravity. Therefore, a person ascending from the surface of the Earth, where the effect of gravity becomes reduced, will lose weight. Ask your students how they would go about finding the point at which a person of average weight would weigh one kilogram less than on the Earth's surface.

Using an old hatbox

"I never hoarded stuff before I became a teacher and now I can't walk past a waste paper bin without looking in!"

Encouraging playful, open-ended, creative responses to problem solving and allowing self-direction are important features of work presented to gifted and talented students. Challenge them to develop confidence in their individual ability as well as to hone their critical analysis skills.

Tell your students about John Logie Baird (1888–1946) who was a Scottish engineer and inventor of the world's first practical, publicly demonstrated television system. Baird built what was to become the world's first working television set using an old hatbox, a pair of scissors, some darning needles, a few bicycle light lenses, a used tea chest, some sealing wax and glue that he purchased in Hastings, East Sussex, along with a few more technical items.

Provide each student with 12 unrelated and random objects. Invite them to first identify a problem that they either have in their every day lives, or a more universal world problem, then ask them to invent an object with the resources you have given them that will solve this problem, just like John Baird did.

Using the idea of the critical friend invite your students to discuss and appraise each other's inventions. Students can suggest improvements or extensions from the inventions.

Teaching tip

It is always a challenge to remain the guide when there is an opportunity to influence activities. Apart from giving practical advice or seeking advice on material handling from other students, restrain your natural instinct to direct thinking. Stand back, make suggestions carefully and work to increase the confidence in the ideas students have for themselves rather than to please you.

Selling the Moon

"'Thinking about it' said Stefan; 'a thing is only worth what someone will give you for it'."

Able, gifted and talented students possess a very high sensitivity to humour and often this is appreciated alongside an understanding of human behaviour. It would intrigue the able mind to research the language of selling.

Estate agent English is a wonderful language in a class of its own. While still telling the truth, it must persuade and seek to maximise the features of what is being sold and minimise the less attractive issues, features and problems associated with the sale. It must do this and keep a professional integrity.

Collect together examples of different forms of estate agent descriptions from mass marketing and exclusive property sale marketing. Ask your students to consider the language used in the selling and description of properties.

- Are there patterns to language use?
- Are there key words used to persuade?
- What conclusions do the students come to about estate agent language?

After all their discussion and thinking, questioning and consideration, ask students how they would expect an estate agent to sell the Moon.

Taking it further

Invite an estate agent into school to talk with your gifted and talented students. It would be interesting for them to hear about persuasive language both spoken and written. How do estate agents present the best feature of a property to help sell it? How carefully do they calculate the effect of their clothing on clients? With the right estate agent this would be a seriously interesting session.

Why do spiders have eight legs?

"A good idea is one that, like a pebble in water, starts waves that go on and on."

Sometimes the most obvious of questions leads on to the most complicated of discussions, projects and assignments. Sometimes a lifelong interest can be sparked by an apparently simple observation.

Why are there no animals with three, seven or nine legs? Animals and insects, crustaceans, birds and anything else you can think of that walks about generally have two, four, six or eight legs.

Ask your students to speculate about why most creatures that move would appear to do so using an even number of legs. The kangaroo hops on two, human beings run, walk, swim and sometimes strut on two legs, as do ducks. Spiders have a generous abundance of legs being usually eight in total. But why? Ask your students to come up with reasons why there are no animals, birds, insects or other living creatures to our knowledge with three or seven or nine legs. Surely a tripod arrangement would be more stable for a giraffe?

Teaching tip

You can be absolutely sure that someone in your gifted and talented group will never cease the search for a three-legged sloth (toes don't count) or 29 legged scorpion just to make a point. Treat this devotion to research as a positive thing.

Birthday swap

"One of the challenges when working with very able children is sometimes getting them to see another person's viewpoint."

This idea is simple. It is about mixing things up, developing research skills and demonstrating synergistic thinking without mentioning that particular word.

Teaching tip

This idea could result in a wide range of outcomes, some serious, some lighthearted. You could have wide-ranging discussions which are interesting and come to a natural stop or you could find yourself eating Lord Roger cake after arranging access to a food technology area. The best advice is to let things develop and see what happens.

Henry Ford, (car manufacturer), Thomas Sowell (economist), Arnold Schwarzenegger (actor and governor of California), Casey Stengel (American baseball player), and Emily Brontë (writer) all share the same birthday, July 30th.

Invite your students to consider what kind of car Emily Brontë would design and make. What kind of novel would Arnold Schwarzenegger write set in Haworth?

Alternatively, ask your students to research five people who have or had birthdays on the same day as themselves, they don't have to be well-known. Ask them to write down the name of a person on one slip of paper and the main achievement of that person on another slip of paper. Then shuffle the two separate sets of paper slips and get each person asked to draw one name slip (for example: Leonardo da Vinci) and one achievement (for example: three successive number one hit songs in the USA).

In this way a creative mix can be produced for general discussion i.e. what hit songs would Leonardo da Vinci be likely to have written? This is a stimulating activity, fun and silly which may well turn up some interesting and challenging ideas for example a cake made Lord Rogers (architect) and a building designed by Mary Berry (baker and writer) would be interesting.

Jokes and geography

"I never tell jokes to my students; they never laugh and it's embarrassing."

Get your students joking! Try the two ideas below to give your students a fresh perspective on geography, in a light-hearted way.

As inhabitable landmass comes under threat from rising sea levels, new land could be created on the oceans. Ask your students to consider when the new land areas are populated, what jokes the people who live in the new ocean surface towns and cities would tell. First, they will have to decide on the geographical features that any new land mass will exhibit.

Terry Pratchett created Discworld with endless opportunities to examine and experience humour. Invite your students to create a new island upon which communication between the island inhabitants takes place only through jokes and puns. It would be fun to create a name for the new islands or continents and publish a collection of jokes created there. The book could be designed and published by students and sold. The profits could then be given to a charity of their collective choice. This is a very demanding idea and perhaps the best way to start would be by asking students to write a single geography lesson using jokes and puns.

Teaching tip

Humour is a dangerous thing to be involved with. It is usually best to stay clear of telling jokes if possible but it's certainly ok to let students play with ideas and share jokes. Be clear however, that the discussion is no place for offensive material of any kind. Stating parameters is always a good idea, as is sticking to what you have said and agreed with your students. Consistency is vital to effective teaching.

Be the first to have a settable!

"I love my chairshelves of power. I feel all-powerful sitting up here."

Broken information exercises such as a mixed-up sentence can be quite good fun. However the game of missing link is even more enjoyable and has the benefit of presenting a creative challenge as well as a problem-solving one.

The evolution of furniture is a rewarding focus for study, consider for example, how the modern chair evolved and developed from a fallen tree or tree stump. The development of furniture involves practical, design and aesthetic appreciation to yield practical, usable and well-designed objects.

Ask your students to think of and then sketch two items of furniture. Further, ask them to describe the main and subsidiary purposes of each item of furniture. The great thing is that it does not matter what they describe by drawing and writing.

Now ask them to imagine a piece of furniture that was the missing link in the evolution from one to the other. For example what piece of furniture, no longer seen, was made that was part table and part settee as one grew into being the other? What would this piece of furniture be called? A settable?! Ask your students to design and draw their answers or suggestions. If time and materials are available then a maquette or even a full-size version of their creations would be an exciting and original object of furniture to manufacture. It would quickly become a must-have piece of furniture for the collector of such things.

Things buried beneath

"I buried all my toys one summer after reading about archeology."

Archaeology is a nice big subject but it's usually not found in any mainstream curriculum. Both these factors make it interesting to the gifted and talented student. When you add the delightful complication of uncertainty about the meaning of artefacts then a very attractive mix of intellectual pleasures hits the student full on.

Introduce this activity with a question. What do you think is under the ground beneath the building you are in? Enrich the question with some added information or thoughts and let the speculation grow.

Things buried under car parks include the remains of the monarch Richard III who was found in Leicester recently and the remains of the warship HMS Glatton under Dover Ferry Port. Ask students to think of their nearest car parks. What do they imagine is buried below them? This idea can then be developed into a discussion as to what is buried beneath their feet, their home, the town, village or city they live in and then further discussion and speculation as to what could be buried under famous buildings and visitor attractions. Develop the discussion by asking your students why they think particular things are buried under particular buildings?

Rescue archaeology is exciting. Task your students with finding the nearest rescue site to your school. Arrange a visit at the weekend or during the holidays. It really is fun and compulsive. You could also consider adopting an archaeological site.

Teaching tip

Always make sure that you have sufficient knowledge about the main content of any activity you are introducing. You don't need an expert level of knowledge, just enough to answer the obvious questions and steer your students in the most positive directions with a feeling of confidence. If you don't find something interesting why should your students?

Taking it further

The disposal of rubbish in landfill sites is an issue worth exploring with your students. What do your students think should be buried beneath the ground if not rubbish?

The optimistic duck

"I find the best way to help an upset child is to give them a rabbit to look after."

Researching the behaviour of living creatures is challenging and means examining both ethical and moral issues, as well as deciding on the most appropriate research methods.

At an animal sanctuary in Kent, scientists from the University of London have been researching the recovery rates and processes that animals use to recover from neglect and cruelty. One of the experiments they conducted was to test and measure optimism or pessimism as demonstrated by the behaviour of goats responding to hidden food rewards.

Ask your students to imagine they have been awarded a research grant of £300 to research the idea that ducks are instinctively optimistic. How would they go about this research?

All you need to do is introduce this idea, and encourage discussion and listening. See where the conversation and discussion leads everybody. When you are concluding the discussion, ask your group what they realised they didn't know about how to carry out a research project.

Extend the discussion by asking students to consider whether it would be in the interest of human beings to ascertain if plants could be classified by human characteristics such as optimism or pessimism?

Knowing our place in creation

"All I know is that everything is amazing."

Gifted and talented students like big complicated ideas. Present them with complex concepts, as in the idea that follows, structured as a collection of interlinking considerations to enable able learners to manage complexity.

Tell your students they are going to have the opportunity to discuss the state of everything! This should interest them. What do they think are the main problems the world faces? Why do we have these problems and what can be done about them? When you feel it is an appropriate moment, ask them to listen while you read this quotation from the book of Genesis:

Then God said, 'Let us make man in our image, after our likeness. And let them have dominion over the fish of the sea and over the birds of the heavens and over the livestock and over all the earth and over every creeping thing that creeps on the earth.' Genesis 1:26

Ask your students to consider what you have read. What do we understand to be the meaning of Genesis? Do we have dominion over *all* things? Let the conversation develop and at the right moment introduce the idea that the word dominion can be interpreted in two ways: as meaning the mastery of everything and alternatively being understood to mean stewardship. Would the world be different if instead of interpreting the word dominion to mean mastery of everything, people understood the word to mean stewardship?

Teaching tip

When managing a complex discussion your anxiety may be high. Relax, be calm, students will talk if you are serious about listening. If they ask questions they are only seeking clarification.

Bespoke teaching

Part 3

Prepare them for the future

"We've designed a lift that takes you into outer space."

Ask yourself which tools and skills your gifted and talented students will need to ensure that in the future they become self-guiding, independent learners.

Teaching tip

Always listen to what your students are really saying to you. Often with new ideas they are seeking an understanding of their own ideas and emerging needs. Act as a guide and support when helping your students understand their own creative thinking. Importantly be a facilitator – not everyone will appreciate the learning needs of the students you support and work with.

While focuses in general teaching life include ensuring exam success and assignment completion, this is not the main focus when teaching gifted and talented students. The gifted and talented child is, more than most people, living in a world that they are developing and making and you must ensure that you help them to prepare for the future by:

- Teaching them to trust their own thinking.
- Developing their critical thinking skills.
- Helping them to explore ethical and moral issues.
- Encouraging them to see doubt as a positive feature of creative thinking.
- Supporting the development of their critical thinking, questioning of accepted ideas and presumptions about what is known about the world.

All of the above are only possible when a safe learning environment exists. The key focus in supporting the learning activities of the gifted and talented student is to keep in mind the time when they will be in charge of their own learning and making sure you prepare them for this time.

Dual exceptionality

"I write a lot of poetry but it all needs translating into proper writing."

The term 'dual exceptionality' refers to those students who are gifted and also have a disability.

Commonly, the description of dual exceptionality refers to learning difficulties such as dyslexia, although it can include a physical disability. When children with dual exceptionality are not properly identified, they do not get the appropriate support they need for either their disability or their giftedness. If we consider a gifted student with an undiagnosed disability, they may appear to be an average performance student.

The effect of any disability on a gifted student's learning is highly complex. If a student has a hearing impairment it reduces considerably their ability to respond to oral direction, discussion and associated learning procedures. A student with a speech or language processing difficulty will not be able to develop an enriched vocabulary with which they can express highly complex thoughts.

Look out for a mismatch between what you feel should be happening with a student and what is actually happening. When in doubt consult medical records and information the school holds, suggest medical assessments with regards to physical disability, and work with your SENCO to test for learning or other possible disabilities or barriers to learning.

Teaching tip

Never let ability or disability mask the rich picture of your student. We should always see the student as a person first, assess their specific needs and help them achieve their best. Increase your own understanding of the student by talking with them, listening to how they feel, what they aspire to, what they really find difficult and then together you can make plans for success and seek out the best routines, support and resources for your mutual sense of achievement.

ADHD

"We are careful about his food but he has started stealing chocolate from shops."

Attention Deficit Hyperactivity Disorder (ADHD) describes significant difficulties either of inattention or hyperactivity and impulsiveness manifesting in the day-to-day activities of a person.

The characteristic behaviour of an able, gifted and talented student with ADHD would include a much greater movement activity level than other children, excessive talking, poor attention levels, an extreme sensitivity to criticism and a noticeable difficulty in adhering to rules and regulations. It is a condition that is both hard to miss and easy to mistake as a part of another behaviour. It requires extreme patience and skill to manage.

Develop consistent routines for learning while being aware that changes in a routine may cause confusion and a challenging reaction from your student. It will help you both if you seat your student near you and try to keep to a minimum his or her ability to see other students during class time. Avoid introducing distractions such as letting the student sit near a window. Noise can also prove very distracting for a student with ADHD. It is important to maintain eye contact when explaining things and setting tasks, keep directions clear and concise.

A student with ADHD should have an individualised support plan for all subjects so that teachers are aware of why the student behaves as they do. Work with your SENCO to prepare and disseminate the plans.

Learning disabilities

"I love starting new things, it's exciting."

The key to developing gifted and talented students with learning disabilities is to harness their imaginative and insightfully creative approach to anything they are asked to do.

While gifted and talented students with learning disabilities will exhibit a wide range of interests and an extensive, developed vocabulary, they may also show a failure to complete extended assignments. Disorganised and often sensitive to criticism, they can often be very good at defining a problem and applying problem-solving skills using their high abstract reasoning abilities. With this in mind why not ask the student how to solve the problem of someone who never completes their assignments?

The usual areas of excellence for gifted and talented students with learning disabilities are geometry, science, arts and music. They have high levels of spatial awareness and good visual memories. They will respond well to the ideas and activities in this book that introduce humour and the need for understanding and deciphering complex systems. Focusing on career options that utilise these skills will allow them access to seeing and exploring challenging and complex work options which will in turn support both their individual development and also their motivation to complete tasks and assignments.

Teaching tip

Gifted and talented students with learning disabilities will often require assistance with sequential tasks. This is an important area to concentrate on to help your students. Jigsaws have a completion challenge, can be pleasurable to complete and require an ordered approach to successful completion. Setting jigsaws for homework might work in supporting your student, try it and see!

Hearing impairment

"Talking louder doesn't help me."

Identifying hearing impairment learning difficulties should always be done by a specialist in the field of the particular area of concern. Never go it alone, always seek help and support.

Many able, gifted and talented students who are hearing impaired will demonstrate a good sense of humour, high reasoning ability, ingenuity when problem solving and will have a wide range of interests. They will also show an early ability to read and have excellent memories. The able student will also be able to negotiate the interpretation of speech without instruction and function well in social situations. The education of hearing impaired students is generally viewed from two distinct viewpoints, the medical model and the social model.

The medical model views hearing impairment as a disability which needs treatment. The social model views the hearing impaired as belonging to a minority but distinct linguistic group.

Professionals and groups who can help you help your students include:

- Consultant audiologists who will carry out hearing tests. The audiologist will also monitor a student's hearing to make sure that any aids are appropriate.
- Speech and language therapists.
- Teachers of the deaf who may be based in schools or operate as peripatetic teachers of the deaf.
- Specialised social workers.

Physical disabilities

"I've learnt to look at getting the big things right."

Self-criticism and perfectionism are particularly characteristic of the gifted and talented student with physical disabilities.

There is a view that gifted and talented children who have a physical disability show a well developed degree of curiosity about the world they live in. It may be that asking the question 'how could the curious cat be saved?' would appeal to them and provide some self-reflection for their own sometimes risk-taking behaviour.

The gifted and talented student will develop compensatory skills, be exceptionally able at problem-solving, be highly motivated and constantly show a highly developed sense of humour. Gifted and talented students with physical disabilities are usually highly motivated, patient and persistent at mastering a skill or knowledge.

Gifted and talented students with physical disabilities may have difficulty with abstractions. In this area they will need extensive support and help from you and their other teachers. Once they have an understanding of a concept they will rapidly grasp an idea and how it can apply to other areas of their learning and knowledge of the world around them.

Teaching tip

Setting unrealistic targets which, when not achieved, are then regarded as a sign of failure can damage to a serious extent the self-worth and self-esteem of a student with physical disabilities. Always offer a perspective on achievement and perceived failure. Is good enough a perfect result? This could be an interesting discussion starting point. As perfectionism is an issue for gifted and talented students with physical disabilities you may want to read Idea 29 Perfectionism.

Visual impairment

"Just because I can't see what's happening doesn't mean I don't know what is going on."

Always be guided by your visually impaired student, often they have more to teach you than you have to teach them regarding resilience, humour, self-discipline and ambition to achieve.

Teaching tip

Never hesitate to work with others from different agencies to support and understand a student with visual impairment. Visit the RNIB website, a charity dedicated to supporting blind and partially sighted people www.rnib.org.uk/. Learn how to read Braille www.wikihow.com/Read-Braille.

The gifted and talented student with visual impairment will often show persistence and application to task completion and high achievement. They will typically demonstrate the following traits:

- A highly efficient memory.
- A highly developed vocabulary and verbal communication skills.
- Persistence.
- A fast rate of learning.

Gifted and talented students with visual impairment will often demonstrate a fast rate of learning and knowledge awareness utilising their unusually highly-efficient memory capability. In addition to being very able at problem solving they may also be very good verbal communicators and possess an extended vocabulary beyond their peers. In some areas of creative application and thinking they may make slower progress than their peers, however they will persist through to task completion. Generally speaking, the able student with visual impairment will master Braille quickly.

In addition, the gifted and talented student with visual impairment is usually highly motivated to know and understand subjects and areas of knowledge, expertise and skill. Although they sometimes demonstrate a slower cognitive development capacity than sighted students they may possess an ability to concentrate with more effectiveness than sighted peers.

Acceleration

"My friends all understand that I like harder work, because they are my friends."

Acceleration is when a student is moved through the curriculum more quickly than their peers.

Acceleration is a powerful approach to sustaining the challenge and pace of learning for the gifted and talented student. If an able, gifted and talented student is not presented with a challenging level or rate of learning they may become bored and disengage with learning. Acceleration has to be carefully judged and evaluated as being the right thing for the individual involved. There should be no pressure to accelerate and acceleration should only be considered with very able children. Difficulties can emerge if the individual's personal, physical, social and emotional well-being is not carefully considered. Able, gifted and talented students do not come in one size or with one set of dispositions; they have very distinct learning needs and should be carefully monitored and supported if acceleration is tried.

Mathematics is usually seen as the area where acceleration can work most effectively, though there is no reason why acceleration should not take place in any subject, providing that everyone involved believes that the benefits of appropriate intellectual challenge will not come at the price of physical and emotional problems that may occur through working with older students.

The question is, however, as the mentor and teacher of a gifted and talented student, how would you ensure the accelerated student could maintain relationships with his or her peer group? This is considered further in idea 42.

Teaching tip

The parents, the student and the teacher working with the student in an advanced setting must all be comfortable with the idea of acceleration. Research strongly supports the value of carefully planned and managed acceleration for able pupils.

Perfectionism

"She's up all night working on her assignments, nothing's ever good enough."

Perfectionism in the context of the gifted and talented student is where the student sets unrealistic achievement and approval levels whereby they ensure failure.

It is very important to help the gifted and talented student who has perfectionist attitudes to realise that perfectionism is not a desirable stance as it does not result in significant productivity or achievement. Perfectionism can prevent even acceptable productivity and desirable outcomes.

Ironically, the seed of perfectionism is that the student has learnt in early life that they are valued for their achievements. The source of their individual self-esteem is therefore outside their control and subject in their eyes to the approval of significant others, such as teachers and parents.

The perfectionist lives with several fears and anxieties such as a fear of disapproval and making mistakes, with rigid rules that guide what is regarded as demonstrating success, and ultimately with a fear of failure. Because of the complex nature of perfectionism in the context of working with the gifted and talented, it can be extremely difficult to manage and resolve. The student sets unreasonable targets, these targets are not achieved, a sense of failure reduces the individual's senses of effectiveness, their productivity is reduced and because they have failed, they become self-critical because they believe they have not tried hard enough. At this stage the cycle continues as more impossible targets are set and the cycle repeats itself and reinforces the pathology.

The underachiever

"The breakthrough was when I found she liked science fiction."

Underachievement is a complex cloak wrapped around a student which prevents them performing and achieving in a positive way.

Underachievement may be caused by school-based concerns, home-based issues, mental well-being issues or a mixture of all the experiences of the student who is underachieving. Work with the student, their family and health professionals to eliminate any obvious issues before moving onto issues such as appropriate challenges, the management of pressure, low self-esteem and depression.

Underachievement can be considered serious enough to require intervention if:

- The student does not achieve anticipated levels of achievement.
- The student is not realising their potential.
- The student demonstrates low self-esteem where they do not see themselves as clever. This can be evidenced as not contributing to discussions or in more extreme physical ways including self-harming.
- The underachievement is a pathological element of the individual's school life.
- Underachievement can be indicated by factors such as: blaming others for problems, declining performance, bullying, poor social skills, lack of motivated engagement in all activities, disorganisation and a preference for oral work.

It is important to always remind yourself that the underachieving student, gifted or not, when appropriately motivated within a safe learning environment can achieve high standards. The state of underachievement can be managed in a positive way and with care is redeemable.

Teaching tip

Use a student's interests to broaden out and address the issues they are managing. The interest may be one that offers social isolation, working at a safe distance from others. Whatever their interest, link it to another subject or skill area such as for example war gaming with the psychology of team management, the biographies of military leaders and strategists, or the mathematics of probability.

Enrichment ideas 2

Part 4

Global migrants

"What I want to be hasn't been invented yet."

It is difficult to advise very able people about their future careers. It is the case that many gifted and talented students go down the university path and succeed; it is also true that many gifted and talented students will invent their own and, to a certain extent, our future.

Every country in the world has a shortage of doctors and nurses. Some countries such as Sweden have an additional shortage in the work force of psychologists.

It is very interesting to think about the chance to explore the changing nature of global economics and the development of new technologies and services, which will create employment opportunities. Ask your students to consider what professions will be required in ten, twenty, fifty years time. Where will these opportunities occur and why? Having discussed the future of work and global economics, ask your students to consider whether the development of technology will reduce the number of jobs available to people. Will there be a need to create new models of work-leisure-volunteering pathways for people in the global economy?

You could invite your students to create their own action life plan with their future imagined profession or job in mind. If a student imagines there will be a need, for example, to have trained professional outer-space detritus collectors, what training and qualifications will they need to follow in order to prepare for that job? This will help them see future planning as a useful skill.

Dramatis personæ

"I love improvisation; you never know where your play will go."

It is a characteristic of gifted students to have a highly developed sense of humour and understanding of language. This idea helps gifted and talented students develop and put these skills into practice creatively.

Start by asking your students what their favourite plays, dramas, or comedies are. Get to know your students' likes and dislikes. Set them the difficult challenge of taking an existing play and introducing at least one new character into it, then working through the play rewriting it, adding in the effect and consequences the new character would have on the plot and other characters.

Allow the writers to develop the character as they wish. Gifted students often have a deep sense of humour and an appreciation of the absurd. They also often have a sense of empathy towards the situations of others, which means the new character (or characters) could be comic or dramatic, or both.

This is a big challenge and won't be done quickly. It is suitable for use as a project over several weeks with development time, rehearsal and readings as part of the extended idea.

Teaching tip

Generally gifted children adore all aspects of drama whether it is writing, acting, prop production or performing. You can act as advisor and arbitrator over decisions. It is perfectly legitimate to simply protect the space for your students to work while they learn through creating.

Taking it further

Use this idea as a competition to find new directors. Once the script with the additional character has been finalised, invite students to present to a panel of judges how they would individually interpret the play and seek to present it. The judges choose the director they feel is most suitable. The real question of course, is who are the judges to be? A problem for your students to solve.

Bad breath/good breath

"How do you politely tell a teacher they have bad breath?"

This activity offers an opportunity for the less socially-able student to witness the more diplomatic students' approach to sensitive issues.

For many students, teachers' bad breath or halitosis can be a serious issue. This is a subject that is not often discussed openly. Be brave!

Sometimes it is a challenge for the able mind to develop diplomacy as often there seems little point in not being straightforward in saying what is thought. Great puzzlement can follow the best of intentions.

Bad breath is a common problem; about one in four people has bad breath on a regular basis. For teachers, bad breath is usually caused by a condition called dry mouth. Teachers talk a lot and unless they drink a lot of water their saliva is reduced, allowing bacteria to build up and causing bad breath.

The questions to ask your students to consider are, what constitutes good breath and what does it smell like, if it has a smell? It would be interesting to conduct an experiment whereby different types of breath could be experienced and the reactions by students tabulated, for example, breath after eating mints or drinking a cherry cola. Are there breath smells that people like? When they have completed their research they can compare their findings with proprietary mouthwashes and breath freshener products.

Taking it further

Build on this idea by getting students to develop a teacher mouth spray range tailored to each of their teachers' subjects. Your students should discuss what maths, French and science smell like, and in what ways they differ. They should research the concept, develop solutions, trial the product, start a company and watch sales rocket!

Arctic greening

"Something will happen. We may not like it but something will happen."

Developing an appreciation of deadlines and grasping the essentials of an argument helps prepare the gifted and talented mind for independent learning.

Give your students a week's warning (or ideally a half-term holiday) that you are going to discuss the topic of species development in the Arctic. This will give them time to read and research the topic so that they can discuss their ideas and the issues involved with an informed viewpoint. You should not need to do any preparation for this activity whatsoever.

Some species of birds that seasonally migrate from lower latitudes and rely on finding particular polar habitats, such as open space for ground nesting will suffer as the Arctic greens. Ask your students, as the Arctic warms up how would they expect it to change? What are the reasons for their suggestions?

Further the discussion by asking your students to consider what characteristics and growth preferences they might expect creatures and plants to evolve with to maximise the benefit of the greening of the Arctic.

Information: Scientists have described 1.9 million species living on Earth. If bacteria are added to the total estimated number of species then the number of species on Earth is 10 million or so.

Teaching tip

Monitoring students and helping to keep them on track with projects is a wise use of your time. It is good for students to know you are interested in them. It is also a good idea to identify problems and issues at the earliest stage possible to make them easily manageable rather than create a crisis.

Bonus idea

Terraforming is a developed science and NASA has plans in place for hugely ambitious programmes where planets with the potential to become new habitats for our species can be made like Earth. What changes would your students suggest that would improve the new Earths? Would the changes they suggest have noticeable side effects?

Future milestones

"I don't really know if I want to go to university. What will I get out of it except debt?"

This idea encourages students to consider their own future and consider how they need to plan for their desired future achievements.

Milestones can be used to reassure travellers that the proper path is being followed and to indicate the distance travelled or the remaining distance to a destination. The milestones of history are key moments where progress or significant change has occurred such as the Battle of Trafalgar (21 October 1805) or the landings on the Moon by Neil Armstrong and Buzz Aldrin (20 July 1969).

Invite your students to consider the milestones of the future. Ask them to consider how the world might be and what the condition of the human species might be in the year 3000. What major future events will be seen as significant advances or turning points that will be regarded as progress milestones between now and when people look back from their future perspective in the year 3000?

Ask each student to choose a particular milestone of the future and produce a detailed history of that event. The future event could be beneficial to our species or catastrophic, in either case ask your students to think about how they would manage to increase the influence of the good event and decrease the influence of the bad milestone.

Your students could produce a futures timeline for display in the school. Space should be left for people to add their thoughts and ideas.

A Narnia of wardrobes

"They aren't really talking, you know."

A playful activity to develop creativity and imagination.

A collective noun is the name of a group of people or things. For example, in the phrase 'a pride of lions', *pride* is the collective noun. There are many websites devoted to the collective noun, for example, http://www.ojohaven.com/collectives/.

Invite your students to make a list of completely unrelated nouns then ask them to create collective noun descriptors for each word on their list, a Narnia of wardrobes, a dearth of bees, perhaps? Most gifted and talented children enjoy word games and nonsense. Ask students to collate an A to Z of new, revised or modernised collective nouns.

Nervous behaviour

"He showed he was bored by never looking at me."

Personal effectiveness skills are those skills needed to take responsibility for developing and managing yourself to improve your personal and professional performance.

Ask your students to work with each other to be hypercritical friends and produce an individualised improvement programme to increase personal effectiveness. Personal body language can involve how a person looks at another, how close they stand to a person, and how they nod at a person.

Invite students to evaluate each other's presentational skills and abilities. Your students should either observe a set-piece presentation on any topic of a student's choosing or simply record their actions through observation during an agreed time. When they have completed the observations let them meet to discuss and evaluate their observations of each other.

New research reveals that nervous behaviour like scratching, lip biting and face touching can serve to relax men and allows them to perform to the best of their abilities in interviews. It is thought to have exactly the opposite effect on women. Give your students the opportunity to research and assess the evidence for this claim.

My lucky pen

"Some students had so many lucky cuddly toys there was no room for the exam paper. I'm glad we banned them."

Learning to research is a key part of the development of the able, gifted and talented student. This idea will develop their ability to interrogate data and draw conclusions.

Students often turn to lucky charms or rituals to help them feel more assured about their exams and to manage stress and uncertainty. 65% of students in a related survey said they were superstitious, with 33% becoming even more so as exams approach.

Some students use lucky pens, wear lucky jewellery, have lucky soft toys of all descriptions, lucky pencils, lucky food and lucky rituals. Logically, lucky charms should be no substitute for well-planned revision but how do we know if this is true? Ask your students to carry out the research below:

- Survey the school to see what percentage of students have lucky charms or rituals during exam time.
- Record and classify the different types of charms and rituals.
- Examine the research findings to establish if any commonality exists with the different charms or rituals.
- Make a schedule of as many lucky charms and rituals as possible, designed to pack in every lucky aspect gleaned from the research.
- Set up an examination for a test group, letting one half of the group use the lucky charms or rituals and the other half take the same exam but without any luck.

> **Teaching tip**
>
> Your own research skills are going to be valuable here. This is a complicated idea and it may be useful to provide a session on research skills and how to examine data.

Identity

"If our history of exploration is anything to go by, aliens may not be in a hurry to make friends."

In a rapidly-changing environment this idea looks at how we might build diplomatic relations between our own species and other species.

How we will or should develop in the future is a serious question given that we are increasingly able to grow flesh, develop artificial organs, control computers and robotics by wireless and generally move toward human design technology. Who are we, what are we going to become and how do we keep ethical pace with these changes?

From sika deer to American crayfish, invasive species are upsetting the natural order of ecosystems on land and sea. The normal human response to invasive species is to determine if they are tasty, or at least edible. Once this has been determined, we eat the edible ones. This approach is one applied to several other key species, which in turn means that as a species they have a high survival rate. The chicken is a real survivor species as a consequence of being tasty and relatively easy to produce on a large scale. More than 50 billion chickens are raised annually.

But imagine what could happen if aliens from outer space arrive and we are the tasty things? How can we de-delicious ourselves? Or like the domestic chicken, should we make sure we are very tasty, useful and attractive so that we are prized as a species? How should we work with other species and other members of our species to ensure survival?

Break it down

"I find it very difficult to think of more than five oranges."

Many gifted and talented students need guidance on identifying the best approaches to prioritising action.

The average human brain contains approximately 100 billion neurons. If a sufficient number of these 100 billion brain cells collectively agree on a working solution, things will happen.

Ask your students to choose a problem they wish to solve. Can the problem be broken down into a set of smaller components? Yes! For example, instead of all exams, focus on one particular exam and perhaps focus again onto one particular aspect of that exam, perhaps the essay, which is worth the most marks. Continue this process until the point is reached whereby practical strategies are possible to solve the true, identified problem.

Explain this to your students as a form of brainstorming, making a rich picture to look at and then start to eliminate items from the rich picture. If anyone, for any reason, says an item should be crossed off the picture then cross it off. Very quickly you will be left with only a few items left to focus on, five is usually a good number of options. From this handful of options, a choice for action and prioritised action can be made.

Ask your students to write down as many world problems as they can think of and make a collective list of everything they have written. Assess the list, apply < and > signs to each item to establish which items are more or less important than others. It will be interesting to see what the group collectively feels is the real problem in today's world.

Teaching tip

The important thing for students to remember is that after brainstorming ideas freely those same ideas can be disposed of freely as well. It is a very powerful way of getting to the point of a matter collectively.

Gifted and talented toolbox

Part 5

How to present activities

"It was the first letter from school addressed to me. I've never been invited to anything before."

The needs of your gifted and talented students are different to the mainstream and this should be reflected in the activities they are invited to become involved with.

The essential attributes of any enrichment idea are that it is interesting, challenging and most importantly that it touches the curiosity nerve of the gifted and talented student. Repeating more of the same is the most likely way of turning a student away from exploring ideas. Ideas can often be used as standalone activities that allow for the student's mind to explore new concepts or aspects of familiar ideas seen in a new way.

Ideas can be introduced as elements within different school activities such as science or arts week or careers and enterprise days.

If the idea is good, if the activity is rich then it will allow a young mind to develop thinking, social skills, presentation skills, and offer intellectual development. The essential elements of successful enrichment activities, whether as standalone, differentiated-in-class activities or as an element of personalised learning, is flexibility in planning and delivery combined with intellectual integrity. Working with your students and supporting how they wish to develop an idea allows them to work at the level of challenge they choose.

Groups

"I don't like working in groups. When we have to show our work I never have anything to show because I have told everyone else what they need to do."

Grouping by ability, task, topic or type of challenge can work, however it is not suited to every activity.

For the gifted and talented, a common complaint is that working in mixed-ability groups all the time without differentiation isn't satisfactory. As mentioned in idea 28, accelerating students can mean splitting them up from their peer group so it is important to weigh up the positives and negatives in each situation – is it better to have them working quickly with students they may not know, or risk them being frustrated working at a slow rate, but with their peer group?

When grouping students, ask yourself three basic but key questions:

1 What do you see as the advantages and disadvantages of grouping gifted and talented students together or allocating them to different groups?
2 How will you support the different groups?
3 How will you evaluate the effectiveness of the grouping arrangement?

If you or a colleague decides to run group activities for gifted and talented students always suggest an identified student from your school register brings along a friend they think may enjoy the activities you present. As well as keeping a link to their peer group, this technique you; some students you would perhaps not have identified as gifted and talented, may come out of hiding and show themselves as gifted and talented when provided with this safe environment to do so.

Critical thinking skills

"Critical thinking isn't about minding the gap it's about crossing the gaps by bridge building and making connections beyond the normal way of seeing things."

Critical thinking involves logical thinking and reasoning of a high order. It involves original, innovative and unlikely relationships between areas of knowledge and experience.

Teaching tip

To identify and differentiate within your gifted and talented group ask individuals to classify a random selection of items that you provide which would appear to have nothing in common (for example an onion, a plastic button, newspaper, wristwatch and so on). The accomplished critical thinker will see connections, map connections, forecast and predict other items within the classification network they have proposed and all in an original, thought-provoking way.

Three overlapping areas of intellectual behaviours were classified by Benjamin Bloom (1913–1999): the cognitive, psychomotor and affective. It is the cognitive domain that should be focused on with regard to thinking skills. Within the cognitive domain, six levels were identified by Bloom:

- knowledge
- comprehension
- application
- analysis
- synthesis
- evaluation.

The ability to evaluate information and ideas, to analyse issues and situations and to synthesise experience and knowledge are regarded as higher-order thinking skills. These skills are also considered to be the essential components necessary to support students to become independent, self-directed learners.

Research by Bloom showed that more than 95% of test questions only required students to think at the lowest operational level to recall information. Essential for learning however, is the development and encouragement of the higher-order thinking skills categorised as critical and creative. The gifted and talented student is able to gather and utilise information from a wide range of sources including verbal or written material.

Differentiation

"When I started to differentiate student's work I quickly realised how important it was to regularly review each student's progress and look for changes in their learning style."

Whichever mixture of approaches to differentiation you try, be sure to discuss them with your group of students. It is easy to confuse students when you change the rules.

Differentiation is a complex area for any teacher and needs continuous monitoring combined with flexibility to advantage both the student and the teacher's effectiveness. Approaches to differentiation can be made through:

- Tiered assessment.
- Developing outcomes to specific learning activities which have different levels of expectations for student achievement.
- Academic buyout whereby the student and teacher negotiate individualised tailored content for a student who may additionally have access to specialists in the individual student's interests.
- Offering choices to students about how they steer their route through an activity.
- Using a range of teaching methodologies, in particular to expand the ways in which students are comfortable learning.
- Gender grouping.
- Flexible grouping.
- Mixed groupings.

Whatever you decide to do, differentiation should always be evaluated. Just because somebody somewhere thought you should follow a certain method does not mean it will be the most effective route for you and more importantly for your students.

Higher-order questioning

"The important thing is the question not the answer."

Developing higher-order questioning is a matter of considering the assumptions we make about knowledge, what we teach and how we teach.

Developing critical and creative thinking depends upon asking and exploring higher-order questions. A really good question results in raising more questions, which inform our understanding of what we know, and of much greater interest, guide us to realising what we do not know (and what we did not know we did not know!) Always encourage your students to consider the nature of an answer and the consequences that result from accepting that answer. Higher-order questioning offers students a challenge to their thinking that is as challenging as their intelligence, enthusiasm and experience allows.

Here are examples of different high-order questions, in categories:

- Application question:
  What could we generalise from the Friday absence records for your school?
- Analytical question:
  How would you classify computer games?
- Synthesis question:
  What do you infer from the statements, reported to have been made by Malala Yousafzai?
- Interpretive question:
  Why does Banksy, the graffiti artist, display his art on public sites and not in art galleries?
- Evaluative question:
  In what way would you defend the €100 billion spent over the last 30 years to maintain the international space station?

Producing enrichment activities and opportunities

"I put all of the test papers from the last five years into a file in the library for extension work and no-one has used them!"

Good enrichment puts the fun and challenge back into the daily grind of the core curriculum for the gifted and talented student.

Enrichment should offer an opportunity to extend knowledge and to think about what links subjects together. A narrow subject-specific approach to extension will fail to develop a student's ability in complex higher-order thinking or sophistication in asking questions.

Enrichment activities should be novel and unusual, be challenging but safe, build on and expand existing knowledge while also allowing for originality of expression and research.

Enrichment should offer and require the student to:

- Consider options and different solutions to problems.
- Develop creativity and imagination.
- Use logical and empathetic thinking.
- Work with others to solve problems.
- Tackle intellectual challenges.

Teaching tip

A good place to start producing your own enrichment materials is with something you can enthuse about, know a lot about and have some original resources. Is your favourite university assignment still available to be used as the base for an enrichment activity? Can you incorporate your scuba diving hobby into the classroom?

HELP!

"It makes my head hurt; there's too much to know."

There are a number of different places, people and organisations who can help you when working with gifted and talented students; make sure you make the most of them.

Sometimes it is really useful to speak to someone you can trust for good advice. Below are two organisations who are experienced and committed to helping teachers of able children, the parents of able children and most importantly, able children themselves.

The National Association for Able Children in Education (NACE)
www.nace.co.uk

The National Association for Gifted Children
www.nagcbritain.org.uk

If you need help with furthering your expertise with gifted and talented students there are the usual advisers and private consultants that are in abundance waiting to help, for a fee sometimes. It is, however, easy to miss people in your own school who also have considerable experience and skills in working with highly able, talented and gifted children. Colleagues in both the Physical Education area and Music are very experienced in spotting talent and coaching for success – they know about motivation and managing rehearsal and training programmes. Getting support is all about developing contacts and finding people who face similar challenges.

Homework

"I do my homework in bed at about midnight with a cup of tea and some toast". "Ah that explains it."

Homework can be a very useful enriching activity if used properly and adapted to fit the needs of a gifted and talented student.

While homework received from your gifted and talented students should be marked against the same agreed scheme and criteria as all other students, it is worth asking individual gifted and talented students how they would prefer their work to be marked. Always receiving a high mark monitors the standard of the homework but offers little to encourage, enrich and extend a gifted and talented student's learning experience.

Aim to offer greater depth to homework marking and suggestions for broadening out the student's understanding of the work involved. Suggest further reading, books or articles. Provide additional homework in the form of an extended assignment which is based on an intellectual or practical interest your student may have.

Homework is not a simple matter of either finishing things off or checking understanding. Homework can be about preparing for future learning and opportunities to show leadership qualities and research abilities whilst also developing a range of essential presentation techniques and skills.

Teaching tip

Always collect homework when you say it must be completed by. Never allow those who have not finished more time. The gifted and talented student expects the contract to be honoured. Why should they work hard to meet deadlines when it appears that deadlines are flexible to you?

Taking it further

Set homework that requires a PowerPoint presentation, a video presentation, a task that is presented in a foreign language or through mime. Extend thinking and creativity with all of your students.

At the drop of a hat enrichment

"Its's fun just playing with ideas."

Not all enrichment or differentiated activities need to be major undertakings requiring a lot of preparation or resourcing.

Able children sometimes enjoy a 'light snack' idea that is playful and stimulating. The development of creativity can be supported with little fun ideas as well as more complex nourishment. Here are examples of enrichment questions that will occupy the curious mind and give you a break!

- If oranges were not coloured orange, what colour should they be?
- Think of some impossible things. How did you do that?
- Should traffic lights only have two colours? Which two colours and why?
- If music were a colour, what kind of music would magnolia be?
- What would solve the environmental issue of disposing of used tyres?
- How could you generate an income from your shadow?
- What advantages would there be for a person who could float three centimetres off the surface of the planet?
- How would you calculate the time it would take to send an email to every person who can receive emails?
- Why are apples the size they are?

Never feel that you have to originate all the enrichment work and resources in your school. Share and use everyone else's good ideas!

Is your provision working?

"I hate geography it's just worksheets and internet searches – there's no real learning."

It is important to continually evaluate your gifted and talented provision. Find out what is being done by other teachers as well as what is being enjoyed by your students and find out whether anything can be improved upon.

Keep an up-to-date gifted and talented register, a record of activities provided for these students and student evaluations of differentiated activities both within and out of the classroom. This information, when combined with tracking data available from your school system of gifted and talented students' progress, will provide you with a fully informed overview of the individual student's progress within the gifted and talented cohort in your school. It will provide a guide to the effectiveness of both your provision and the differentiated provision of other colleagues.

If students are making measurable progress as they should be, then it indicates your support and provision are suitably challenging and tailored for your particular student needs. If however progress is poor or inconsistent then examining your records, student evaluations and tracking data will help pinpoint with accuracy and confidence what needs to change or be improved. This might include future provision, target setting, further teacher support, resource requests and improving what you as a school are offering the gifted and talented students.

Teaching tip

Know the experience of your students and monitor it to improve that experience by talking with them, as well as talking to their parents, governors and your colleagues. Build up in your mind an understanding of what they respond to, find challenging and enjoy. You can then advise other colleagues on approaches that will work with individual students in your colleague's subject areas.

Taking it further

Invite your gifted and talented students to devise their own methods for evaluating the quality and suitability of the differentiated enrichment and extension work they are provided with. When they have clarified their ideas see if they can provide a checklist indicating what good enrichment work should always include. This checklist would be a great resource for you and your colleagues when creating enrichment work.

Enrichment ideas 3

Part 6

Healthy cutlery

"Smaller plates make the portions look bigger, everyone knows that."

Sometimes the most ordinary everyday objects and ideas can form the basis of activities that will become major topics of enrichment and even possible career options. With this activity a student could be led into the study of ergonomics, anthropology, psychology, design, food technology and medicine.

Teaching tip

A teaching resource for students does not have to be professionally produced or expensive. Practically anything can become a vehicle for developing thinking skills. Start to look at the curriculum you teach and have a notebook for jotting down the ideas you have as you prepare and review core lesson plans and concepts.

Cutlery did not just happen, it evolved to meet a need, a need that changed over time as the types and frequency of food eating and social eating developed. The fork as we know it emerged in the 18th century. In the West we mostly use the knife, fork and spoon when eating. Modern inventions and changes to cutlery include the spork, which is a combined spoon and fork. The spife, knork and sporf are also combinations of different items of cutlery.

Discuss changing food habits and the possible changes that could be made with cutlery. Ask your students to consider and design an improved item of cutlery that in some way influences what and how we eat in a way that is healthier for us and promotes a healthy lifestyle. The spoon could offer comfort and reassurance in some way or the fork could change colour if the food was bad for your particular health profile. Your students will prove to be inventive once they have grasped the idea of re-designing cutlery to improve the health of eaters. To support their ideas they should be encouraged to sketch their concept cutlery.

The professional development of working with other teachers and facilitators can be incalculable, especially with an activity like this one. See if anyone in design and technology is willing to help your students make their designs into working models.

The Great Game

"It seems to me that there are always wars somewhere."

Big issues are of great interest to the able student. Understanding the complexity of the present world is necessary for developing higher thinking skills and developing the ability to ask pertinent questions.

The term 'The Great Game' is normally attributed to Arthur Conolly (1807–1842), an intelligence officer of the British East India Company's Sixth Bengal Light Cavalry. The term was introduced into popular use by British novelist Rudyard Kipling in his novel *Kim*. It describes the strategic rivalry between the British and Russian Empires for supremacy in Central Asia from the Russo-Persian Treaty of 1813 to the Anglo-Russian Convention of 1907. The term continues to be used as the world's great powers and the regional powers still seek geopolitical influence.

Provide your students with a selection of newspapers from around the world and ask them to read through them, drawing out how they think the relationships are between the major countries in the world. From this initial discussion invite your students to study news programmes on television, the radio and the Internet. Ask them if they can identify patterns in the behaviours of, and between different countries.

At your second meeting, continue the discussion about how and who are the real powers in the modern world. Invite a discussion about what Great Game is being played and is unfolding in the 21st Century.

Teaching tip

In the week before you try this idea ensure that you have time set aside to read newspapers and news reports concerned with international events. You will need to know what you are talking about!

Taking it further

If a particular student or students find this area of study interesting you could suggest they investigate in some depth the life and times of Arthur Conolly. This will inform students as to the historic background of the relationships between the great powers and inform how international affairs are currently carried out.

Parrots in space?

"It's the best thing about here. I see my rabbit every night."

Gifted students enjoy a good metaphysical discussion. The issue of relationships between humans and animals is a vehicle for a discussion about the social and psychological needs of human beings.

Teaching tip

Check that no-one in your group has lost a pet before you present this idea for consideration. Most children feel a degree of loss at the death of a pet, for the able child that sense of loss may be considerable. It is also true that for some able students a very down to earth, pragmatic approach to the loss of a pet could be their reaction.

Taking it further

Ask your students what they think about the concept of banning all pets, of any kind? What would be, if any, the psychological, economic and environmental issues that would need to be considered if such a ban was instituted worldwide? How would a ban be introduced?

Mark Twain is famously reported as saying 'The more I learn about people, the more I like my dog.' Pets in real life as well as in fiction, have strong and important relationships with people, for example the fictional association of pirates and parrots and the real life fact that the writer Beatrix Potter did have a real Peter Rabbit. Your students may have pets of their own; start a conversation about their feelings towards them. Extend this activity by asking your students to consider what likely pets of the future would astronauts, deep space explorers and planet populators benefit from having?

Students can also explore the questions: why would one need a pet in space and why do we have pets at all?

Useful information to help your discussion:

- Pets can help their owners relieve stress and loneliness.
- Pets such as dogs increase their owners' opportunities for exercise and outdoor activities, therefore increasing the opportunities to meet and to socialise with other dog owners, enriching their lives.
- Watching fish swimming in an aquarium has a calming effect and helps lower blood pressure.
- Owning a dog or cat can help lower blood pressure.
- Pets can decrease the owner's cholesterol levels.

Future proxemics

"I hate it when teachers stand right behind me in exams."

It is empowering for gifted and talented students to have an opportunity to study and discuss how people relate to each other in a physical sense.

Proxemics is the study of the cultural, behavioural, and sociological aspects of spatial distances between individuals. Try these exercises with your students to explore and introduce a discussion about proxemics.

Hand shakes. Ask students to face each other and shake hands. They will largely stand about a metre apart, nearer if they know the person well, a little more distant if they don't. What happens if they stand nearer or farther away than they normally would? How do they explain the resulting behaviour? How do they explain the choices they make about where they want to stand in this activity?

Walking backward. In pairs, ask students to stand facing each other at a distance they find comfortable. Then ask one of the pair to walk towards the other partner. What happens? Why do most people involuntarily walk backwards to maintain an equal distance? How can this knowledge be used to manage a bully or to manage a person who is anxious?

Ask students to consider:

- The placing and arrangement of desks and chairs for public examinations. Can they think of any reason for the usual arrangements other than to prevent copying?
- Will, as the world population increases, accepted proxemic behaviour change over the next 25 years? Why do they think their answer is correct?

Teaching tip

Before you try this exercise, watch people in everyday situations. How close do they stand to another person if they like them or dislike them? How and where do people choose to sit in public spaces such as libraries? How close do you like people to stand to you?

Beginning and end

"When you understand the middle bit of a problem everything else is easy."

Many gifted and talented students will become managers either as a full-time occupation or as a part of their main occupation. Management skills are not often taught in schools and this activity is useful in addressing problem-solving and achievement management.

Teaching tip

Promote ambitious thinking through increasing the complexity of the endings to be achieved. Always take the ideas and statements produced by students as serious proposals even suggestions made in jest, for example 'issuing luminous kneecap protectors to all citizens' could easily be paired with an ending like 'no child in the world dies from drinking polluted water'.

Bonus idea ★

Invite your students to discuss and select the top five world problems such as the use of chemical weapons, an increasingly ageing population or child mortality. Using the management rules they devised in the main idea, can they create a process where they can see a possible solution to their chosen problem?

Every moment there is a beginning and an ending. Often the ending is also another beginning. In management terms it is the bit in between that is the interesting challenge.

Invite your students to write down a beginning and an ending. They can be factual or fictional events, something completely random such as 'today I sold my last jar of crab apple jelly', or 'I started my dream job as Owner/Director of the Marine School, Oman' or 'today the last atomic weapon in the world is being decommissioned'. Make pairs with the beginnings and endings. Now, this is the interesting bit, what has to be done from the given starting point to achieving the end point?

Next, ask your students to identify any patterns they can deduce related to problem-solving or goal achievement. Are these observations universally applicable to assisting with problem-solving? Can they establish a set of rules or guidelines for managers to always follow, which would ensure task achievement every time?

The last words written

"We can learn more about how a person thinks and what makes them tick from the words they use rather than the content of their writing."

This idea looks at human emotions and psychological profiles as expressed in literature. Examining these glimpses of thoughts and emotions offers a way into both understanding complex literature at a deeper level and adding to the resources available to the gifted and talented student to consider their own emotional and psychological make up.

Ask your students to research the last written words of people who have died in extreme situations. Is there a pattern to what is written? What do the last words tell us about the writers' state of mind at the time? In your students' judgement, when writing letters to loved ones from terrible situations, is it ever necessary, acceptable or appropriate to tell lies? Is it possible to always be truthful and accurate when speaking and describing the world and a person's inner life?

An example of 'last words' that could be used to introduce this idea is the final letter written by the dying explorer Captain Scott, from inside his final Antarctic camp in March 1912: 'Finally, I want you to secure a competence for my widow and boy. I leave them very ill provided for, but feel the country ought not to neglect them.' It is believed the Antarctic explorer died on 29 March 1912.

Ask your students to write what they imagine would be the last letter that will ever be written if telepathic communication were to be realised. What problems and concerns can they imagine as a result of people being able to read another person's thoughts?

Teaching tip

This what if idea is based well within scientific research and interests. You could provide a selection of copies of last letters for your students to read and discuss. The heavy censorship of letters sent in the First World War would provide good examples and interesting discussion, as many were self-censored.

Taking it further

It would be interesting to experiment with telepathy using Zener cards (cards invented by Karl Zener in the 1930s used to detect extrasensory perception, ESP). This is a good example of developing your students as researchers and self-learners. Ask them to research and make a set of Zener cards. Also ask them to find the protocols for acceptable research methods when carrying out telepathy.

The sailing log of a space traveller

"Bad science in science fiction writing is so bad!"

Combining travel writing, science fiction and fantasy presents a real literary challenge for the young writer especially when the science has to be right as well.

Early travel writers and accounts of exotic exploration such as those by Richard Hakluyt (1552–1616), Freya Madeline Stark (1893–1993) and Colin Thubron, (born 1939) allow us to experience worlds and far away cultures that ordinarily would be impossible for us to imagine.

This idea allows students an opportunity to imagine and play with ideas, it also asks them to be creative with clear parameters of fact. Ask your students to imagine they are a scientist, travel writer and explorer who has been asked to write a 500 word article for *Mars Science Today*. Their writing brief is 'A walk through the Reull Vallis of Mars'. The information below should provide a good start for their article and research.

The Reull Vallis region of Mars shows river-like structures in the images returned to Earth. These structures are thought to have been created when running water flowed on Mars. The rivers would have been powerful enough to cut a dramatic and steep-sided channel through the Promethei Terra Highlands. The river would then drain into huge Hellas basin.

What did Chaucer eat for breakfast?

"I insist on my cooked breakfast as stated in my contract, Headmaster."

Set a surprise weekly challenge. When you meet at the end of the week you can discuss it. Eventually students could provide you with the challenges they had thought of themselves.

A weekly, surprise thinking challenge or activity can be a way of keeping your students on their toes and encouraging them to be curious, ask good questions and develop research skills. Here are some ideas for surprise enrichment:

- What did Chaucer have for breakfast? In the prologue notes to *The Canterbury Tales*, Chaucer (1342–1400) writes that 'people long to go on pilgrimages' in the spring because winter is over, and it's time for renewal.' The days were also getting lighter and warmer and food was increasing in availability and variety. The prologue does not however tell us what Chaucer ate for breakfast; ask your students to find out. Give them one week.

- Why do people in the West traditionally read left to right? Put together a presentation (in a week) to give to the rest of the group.

- What would be the economic effect of the disappearance of honey-bees from the world? Write an article for the local gardening society.

- Who makes the medals that are given to people who receive knighthoods? Extend this research task into one whereby your students are asked to find the cost of such medals and if they could do the manufacturing at a cheaper price.

- Where in Scotland is the village, town or city with the shortest name?

Teaching tip

You do not always need to have your gifted and talented students for long sessions. Nor do you need to spend time working with other colleagues' details of individualised enrichment pathways for gifted and talented students. You could have a weekly challenge, which they pick up from you or the school office at a fixed time.

Bonus idea ★

Invite your students to create their own surprise weekly challenges. The questions can be silly or serious, unusual or deal with the obvious. The point is that they should be unexpected and stimulate thinking amongst their fellow students.

Celebrating a life

"We care about people; it's what we do."

A trait in many gifted and talented students is their high empathy awareness and sense of other people. This idea offers a forum to discuss the issues of bereavement and death.

This idea should be presented with great care. A student may have suffered a serious bereavement recently, or in their lifetime, or there may be students with friends facing severe illness. You must be sensitive to the bereavements your students may have experienced, whether it is loss of a relative, or pet. In a pre-activity discussion approach the group carefully, seeking out any areas of sensitivity and ascertain the individual's readiness to proceed with the activity. If in any doubt do not use this activity, save it for another day.

While the use of confetti at weddings is acceptable it is considered taboo at funerals. With an increasingly ageing population, attitudes to death and funerals are changing. Coffins can now be extremely colourful and individualised by their shapes as well. Often funeral services are viewed as celebrations of the person's life and mourners are asked to remember a person with positive and fond memories. While religious ceremonies may remain formal and a matter of ritual, civil funerals have a great deal of choice as to how they are carried out.

Ask your students how they would seek to innovate funeral proceedings to reflect a changing view of death, funerals and mourning whilst still respecting both the memory of the deceased and their loved ones?

Toponymy

"My study of county place names kept me sane during all the boring other stuff I had to do."

Studying place names helps students make sense of the wider world and how things may change. The gifted and talented mind likes complexity.

Toponymy is the scientific study of place names or toponyms, their origins, meanings and typology. Through place names we can learn about how far invaders reached and settled into countries, agricultural settlements, industrial developments, the economics of a period and the movements of peoples.

Introduce this subject by asking your students if they know why their school is called the name it is called. You will of course need to know this information yourself before you start! Your school may be named after a local or national figure of importance, or named after a local area or even named to inspire confidence and ambition amongst those working and studying there. Take the discussion further to begin a discussion on local street names (the street or road each student lives in is a good point for discussion) and then move on to why the area they live in is called by the name they all know. For example 'Wilberforce Avenue, Hull': why is the avenue called Wilberforce and why is Hull called Hull?

This activity could take the form of a class discussion concerning the naming of things or be developed into a research topic as to what the names of places tell us about the place's history and background. Additionally, as an extended homework or special project for your students you could ask them to examine and research the area they live in, looking at all the names of places in order to produce a map of the area explaining why the names in use are in use and what they represent.

Teaching tip

Know the history of your school's name. Have local maps and gazetteers of your local area ready for this activity. Be ready to suggest an area you have good and detailed maps of so that students can get a feel for the scale of the idea and challenge.

Taking it further

Ask your students to imagine they are tasked with establishing a system for renaming all place names throughout the area they have researched. On what basis would they make the name changes and why?

Embedding the provision

Part 7

IDEA 61

Teacher briefings

"It's really good to hear what is going on in other classrooms and how my students are doing in other activities – sometimes I wonder if it is the same student!"

While it is true that attending school and 'lesson learning' do not appeal to all students, we can be sure that the motivated gifted and talented student is hungry to learn, develops learning and communication skills quickly and above all is enthusiastic about learning.

Teaching tip

Always keep the formal and informal evaluations and reviews by your students up-to-date. As well as the uses mentioned in this idea, these documents are particularly valuable for you as a measure of your developing expertise in the area of providing for gifted and talented students.

The skills that a teacher develops when working with gifted and talented students and the teaching approaches of collaboration and co-learning can be used by all teachers in every class-room and learning situation. Keep a note of what works (and what doesn't) when you are leading activities or introducing ideas with your gifted and talented students. Use these notes to do two important development services for your colleagues that will benefit them in their teaching and in turn help their pupils.

- Staff bulletin notice board: physical (in the staffroom) or electronic (in the staff section of your school intranet). Post a weekly/bi-weekly account of what you have been doing with your gifted and talented students and include a 'Teacher's tip' plus a student comment on an aspect of the lesson or activity they enjoyed (or which went slightly off plan).
- Top and Tale Review: a presentation to colleagues about what you plan to do during a forthcoming term at the beginning of term and another presentation to colleagues at the end of that term as to how things went, what was achieved, what worked, what didn't work and what you did when things didn't work.

Taking it further

The reviews could be within the school formal staff development programme or they could be in the form of an informal lunchtime event where staff are invited to come along. In this way you will be working with colleagues who are interested in developing their skills and importantly are supportive of your work with gifted and talented students.

74

Tactful teaching and listening

"I was a bit worried when you turned up; you had no notes or resources. I don't know why but the group enjoyed just talking all day."

Listening effectively is, for a teacher, a skill that involves a developing relationship between themselves and their students.

All teachers have to have control to protect and to guide learning, as well as ensuring individual and group safety. Classroom control based on mutual respect and openness makes for a powerful, creative experience. The alternative, control by subjugation, is not the best approach to win trust and mutual respect.

Listening and reflecting upon what is said by students offers a valuable source of knowledge and data to help the teacher understand the extent and limits of a student's comprehension of a subject, their ability to self-learn and develops their respect and trust. Showing a willingness to enter into open discussion with students demonstrates a willingness to embrace uncertainty, confusion and risk-taking.

One way of entering into a discussion with your students is to bring to a session a single sheet of A4 paper. It should be prepared with a few notes outlining what you are going to do. Place the paper face down. Give each student a blank piece of paper and ask them to predict what your lesson plan is about, then discuss their predictions. This will be very revealing about the thoughts, ambitions and anxieties your students are concerned with and will make a great basis for discussing what learning is really about. At the end of the session, reveal your lesson plan. It will of course be the lesson plan for the above activity.

Teaching tip

Invite a colleague to sit in on a lesson you are teaching. Ask this critical friend to observe and note down the number of times you did not 'hear' a student comment. After the lesson discuss any missed listening and try to understand the different reasons why some students were heard and others not. This exercise is an incredibly courageous thing to do – but worth it – as your teaching will improve.

Taking it further

It might be fun to develop the lesson plan ideas that your students come up with into lessons you can use with your other students, or you could get them to develop them into lessons themselves that they could run with the rest of the gifted and talented cohort.

Micro enrichment moments

Teacher: "Can anyone suggest an impossible thing to be able to do?"
1st student: "Touch your left elbow with your left hand, Miss."
Teacher: "Yes."
2nd student: "No, you just chop the left hand off and then you could."

Always expect the unexpected; plan in slippy time for unexpected discussion or the exploration of outcomes that you had not expected to occur during the lesson you had planned.

Teaching tip

Make sure that when something unexpected happens in a lesson it is used to enrich and excite learners, for example a collapsed book shelf could be the cue to ask your students if the shock they have just experienced would have been similar to the effects of the fall of the Roman Empire or the Hindenburg disaster?

Taking it further

In the same way that a lesson can offer an unexpected bonus learning point a lesson can offer the student an opportunity to consider what they now don't know! Invite your students to write down on a slip of paper one thing they now don't know about a the subject you have been teaching. Mix the slips of paper up. Let each student choose a slip of paper and they have the task of answering the question for the next lesson.

What have been described as micro-moments of opportunity during the teaching and learning experience within the classroom can also play an important part in enriching the experience of the gifted and talented student. They will have hundreds of ideas, creative, fanciful and impossible. In all lessons there are possible micro-enrichment opportunities that will extend the consideration of the lesson content and encourage creative, lateral thinking by your students. Here are a few examples and ideas to illustrate the concept:

- English: How would the world be different if English was not the most widely used language?
- Mathematics: How probable is it that probability exists as a concept and can be calculated?
- Science: What part does 'luck' or 'guess work' plays in the advancement of science. Can they think of any examples?
- History: What if any was the significance of the hats worn by Wellington and Napoleon to the outcome of the Battle of Waterloo?
- Geography: Would there be a positive reason to revive and induce volcanic activity in the UK?

Sometimes of course the micro enrichment opportunity will come from the students themselves.

How to enrich enrichment

"Now we have drawn the flying train, can we make one?"

When you present an activity or an idea for discussion with your gifted and talented students, many associated ideas and topics will be raised. These ideas can be used as the starting points or seeds for building on and developing, further enrichment ideas or activities.

When the thinking of your students has been stimulated by an idea or activity you have introduced, tangential thinking should be encouraged. A consideration of global warming, for example, and the problems raised for the well-being of and survival of our and other species could lead to asking your students to design a non-leather shoe made from an artificial material which would convert carbon dioxide into oxygen. This task could further lead to students exploring the economic effect of leather no longer being required for the manufacturing of shoes.

The consequences of this train of thought can be further explored; with fewer animals being required to be slaughtered for leather, how would you measure the related fall in gas emissions worldwide due to a reduction in cattle breeding and what would the effect be on grain markets as less grain will be required for animal food, suggesting the possibility that more grain becomes affordable for human consumption? This simple idea of a non-leather shoe emerges as a discussion concerning the long-term effect of the reduction of hunger throughout the world.

Many of the enrichment activities in this collection can both promote and inform discussions and outcomes, which expand and enrich the original proposition.

Teaching tip

While it is a positive achievement to engage your student's thinking to the extent that they get excited by ideas and concepts, develop exotic content in discussion and generally run with an idea, always ensure students complete a finished piece of work if you have asked for it! For some gifted and talented students ideas are as forthcoming as water from a spring; the challenge can be to develop a 'completer-finisher' approach to work. Jumping steps in learning should not come at the cost of ensuring that your students have the skills they need to succeed in realising their potential.

Emotional intelligence

"He's the best prefect for years, he seems to understand what everyone is going to do before they do. There's never trouble or rows when he is around"

Developing an individual's emotional intelligence can help the gifted and talented student become more able to focus, less stressed and importantly to develop an understanding of the intentions, behaviours and priorities of other people.

Teaching tip

Emotional intelligence is an awareness of how your actions and feelings affect those around you. Very often *what* you say is less important than *how* you say it. Examine your own emotional intelligence and look at how you physically interact with students; the way you stand when teaching (what do you think you are saying if you stand behind the desk for example), how loud you speak, whether you look at students and so forth.

Taking it further

Get your students to do a self-evaluation. What are your weaknesses? How can you improve your personal effectiveness through an increased understanding of emotional intelligence?

Emotional intelligence is often associated with the work of Daniel Goleman who identified five domains of emotional intelligence: Knowing your emotions; Managing your own emotions; Motivating yourself emotionally; Recognising and understanding other people's emotions; Managing emotional relationships.

Practical strategies to help your students develop their emotional intelligence include:

- Watching films. Many address areas such as empathy and self-awareness. Discuss with your students a film they felt dealt with the powerful forces of emotional intelligence. Watch the film and discuss what can be learnt about effective communications between people from the ideas and themes within.
- Watching people in different settings. See how people in different situations react to each other. For example, in a public library.
- Ask students to observe how they react to people. Tell them to consider how they interact with others and try to put themselves in their place and be more open and accepting of their perspectives and needs.
- Get students to write a short play about good and poor interactions with people.
- When looking at a play text with your students, get them to annotate the emotional intelligences shown by different characters.

A place to learn

"Everywhere, whether in a classroom, corridor or playground, should be a safe place to learn and grow."

A safe place is calm, has rules and is consistently protecting the right to ask and answer questions in a respectful, critical friend environment.

Health and safety issues are well known when we discuss our physical environment. We are all aware of our duty of care to others and the need to afford each other respect. One important responsibility you have as a teacher or manager in regard to the gifted and talented student is to help them to feel safe in how and where they learn.

Remember to:

- Keep rules to a necessary minimum.
- Make rules clear and concise.
- Make sure what you expect from your students and what they should expect from you is clear.
- Make rewards and punishments a matter of social justice, appropriate and equitable.
- If you say you are going to do something then do it or let your students know why you have changed your plans.
- Never be sarcastic or belittle a student.
- Negotiate authority; it is always best to avoid confrontation or struggles with the gifted child.
- Understand that your students have needs and concerns. Your students are emotionally rich, complex people, respect them.
- When you make a mistake, acknowledge you have done so. It is a great lesson to teach that after a mistake comes improvement and the world generally does not end.
- The right kind of praise can go a long way.

Teaching tip

Invite students to self-evaluate their understanding of classroom success and what a safe environment means for them. Justifying their decisions with others is a way of helping individual students identify problems and solutions with regard to their own status as a learner.

Still just a child

"You can have this," said Peter, handing me a scrappy piece of paper before running off to play football. It was a rather sophisticated analysis of a Keats poem. "Not bad for a 12 year old who had only been introduced to Keats's writing an hour ago", I thought.

High intellectual ability does not exclude the possibility of adhering to convention. No matter what the level of ability a child demonstrates it should never be forgotten that they are young in experience and may upon occasion surprise you by being 'childish'. Relax and let the child be a child.

Always remember that however clever an individual student is, they are a young boy or girl and like all children, they want to play and are as likely to hand you an elegant mathematical observation as talk about hair styles, computer games, badminton, dieting or apps. They may equally be rather focused on a particular subject to the exclusion of anything else and appear to be an adult professor. The point is that gifted and talented students have two things in common with all other children. The first is that they are children with all the issues of children and secondly they like to play. When working with gifted and talented children, don't forget that you are working with human beings and not just IQs.

Who else is on your team?

"Once I joined the British Brick Society I made lots of friends. Not many people are interested in Victorian blue-glazed engineering bricks where I live."

Sharing expertise and resources with others and working together in the provision of support for the gifted and talented is essential.

Cluster groupings, partnerships and extended networks can help you improve provision for your students and develop your own skills and knowledge. Of course, there are the obvious links to be explored with university departments, other schools, both state and private, in this country and worldwide but in addition, local businesses, Rotary associations, libraries and theatre groups can all be sources of inspiration and support. If managed carefully the local media and press can also be useful in providing placements, speakers, tours and visits.

National and local museums will all seek to influence audiences and be anxious to work with identified groups. In addition to local church groups there are sporting associations, voluntary groups and police community link officers who may be able to provide resources.

Teaching tip

Work with other schools to maximise each other's resources. Whether it is a shared art activity or science project it is beneficial to harness the skills of as many people as possible and to reduce the total workload on one person all the time. Ask your students to identify as many local and county groups they can that are for people interested in chess, drama, local history, poetry, sailing, music, flower arranging, armour, fishing, antiques, travel, whatever you can think of. Choose a selection of groups and invite a speaker from each one to present a talk and share some insight into their interests. Make the talks open to all students and staff.

Resources and funding

"I never mention money or amounts I just listen to the reasons I can't have any first."

It would be reasonable to receive some funding from the school budget if you have a responsibility for supporting and managing the provision for gifted and talented students. The question is, how do you justify this when funding is under pressure?

Begin the process of securing the funding you need by increasing the visibility and positive contributions to school life of your gifted and talented activities.

When seeking financial support it is important to:

- know why you want the finance
- show how it will benefit the students and teachers and importantly the school
- present costed and researched alternatives to achieving your aims
- have researched different sources of funding which would compliment any funding that was forthcoming from school capitation. In addition to school capitation and PTA funds there are charities large and small that would want to support good ideas
- be prepared with a prioritised list and an argument for each item
- demonstrate (if possible) a good track record of making the most of any previous funding you may have received
- present how others in your school could benefit from what you propose to do
- be prepared to accept less than you applied for – there are many urgent needs in a school – prepare to make your case and equally be prepared to see the needs of others. Build alliances for the future
- choose your timing carefully – strangely the end of the financial year can expose under-spending – be ready to act quickly.

Making friends with parents and carers

"The best thing about coming to Saturday Club is meeting new people and doing things in a relaxed way."

It is as important that parents and carers understand the needs of their gifted and talented sons and daughters, as it is that school does. Everyone needs to work together.

While it is important to congregate able, gifted and talented students together so that they have a peer group, it is also important to include parents and carers in your work. There are several ways, in addition to the usual school reporting procedures and parents evenings, that you can work with parents and carers to support the gifted and talented students.

Organising parent workshops is a great way to get parents and carers involved. The workshops should be designed to explain how their children think and like to work. For example, on one such evening a parent who was given a maths problem to solve became totally involved with the problem – his daughter was amazed as she had never seen her father 'learning' in an enthusiastic way.

The workshops are also an opportunity for parents/carers to work with their children on common challenges and it can be a hugely positive activity. They need only be presented once a term. They should involve clear evaluation opportunities and welcome ideas for future workshops. Parents/carers often have skills they will wish to share or even offer opportunities to visit unusual and interesting places such as a water-works or rail signal box or a cross-channel ferry (all of which I have been fortunate to visit with different gifted and talented groups).

Teaching tip

Anxiety and attention-seeking behaviour are nearly always present in different degrees when parents get together. You need to prepare carefully for these issues for any workshop your run. Make sure that you know what you want to achieve in the session and have a full programme that keeps people informed and active. Make it clear that you are not running a parents' evening nor are you there to answer questions about policy, funding or any other matter to do with school. You are running workshops to inform parents and carers as to how they can best help their children. One last tip – don't be worried about questions – if you do not know the answer, say so. You can find out or ask your parent/carer group if anyone knows the answer to the question asked.

Enrichment ideas 4

Part 8

The egg of the extinct elephant bird was BIG

"Give a bright child an idea and you never know where it might go."

Exploring ideas where fiction, fantasy and science can be blended together expands the creative thinking of students. Examining and playing with ideas such as the giraffe bird leads to a consideration of the physical and biological attributes of successful and less-successful species.

Elephant birds were large, flightless birds that once lived on the island of Madagascar. They became extinct during the late 17th century.

At 30cm tall and 21cm in diameter, the egg of the elephant bird is about 100 times larger than an average chicken egg, and larger than eggs laid by dinosaurs. An intact egg of the elephant bird was, in April 2013, sold for £66,600.

This activity looks at the possible sizes, design, function and individual features of imaginary birds such as the giraffe bird, the hedgehog bird, the whale bird or any hybrid your students can imagine. Ask students to generate a list of imaginary birds and then work out the practicalities of such a bird. How could the bird fly? How big and what type of wings would such a bird need? How would the bird reproduce? What kind of habitat would the bird find most suitable for living successfully? Would the bird have any predators and if so how would it defend itself?

The one rule with this activity is all features of the bird must be based on existing knowledge, physics and biosciences. With this activity there is no place for magic antigravity toes.

Invisible theatre

"Drama's my favourite."

This idea offers an opportunity to explore the part played in theatre by an audience. Theatre is often seen and experienced as a 'them and us' experience whereby the audience receives a play or production in a passive manner. The work of Boal introduces the exciting idea of the audience and performers experiencing a dramatic event together as a real-life event.

The 'Invisible theatre' was developed by the Brazilian, Augusto Boal and Panagiotis Assimakopoulos who conceived of the concept of the 'Theatre of the oppressed'. His perspective on theatre was that it was social transformative in nature, a form of theatrical performance taking place where people would not normally expect to see a performance. The performers attempt to disguise the fact that it is a performance from those who observe and who may choose to participate in it, encouraging the spectators to view it as a real event.

Invite your students to write an invisible theatre performance to take place in and around their school where the play is run in different areas but as a time-coherent performance. Ask your students to consider who in these circumstances is the audience and who are the actors.

When the locations have been agreed and the play is written, have a go at performing it and recording the performance. It would be extremely exciting to have mobile phones transmitting the performances in real time whereby it could be experienced by the actors and audiences at different locations and become a more traditional event viewed by a collective audience.

Teaching tip

It is not necessary to know where you are going with this activity. Present the idea to your gifted and talented students and see how it develops. Let them discuss the idea and begin to make suggestions. You may need to be the sounding board, health and safety manager and the facilitator for resources, but you don't however need to micro-manage.

Bonus idea ★

Take the idea even further by combining the work of your students with the presentation method of the 'flash mob' whereby an event, unannounced to the general audience/public takes place by performers who as soon as the performance is over blend in with the audience/public.

Just six recipes

"I'm not sure I could eat earthworms."

Food, diet and health are important subjects to explore as they can connect to so many areas of curriculum development and enrichment. The gifted and talented student is able to make complex connections between subject areas. Food connects with mathematics, science, art, economics, chemistry, sociology, English and technology. The subject of food also offers an opportunity to explore social justice, sustainability and well-being issues related to citizenship.

Teaching tip

This activity is typical of good enrichment work, it is based on real world activity, it is a familiar subject to students, there is an interesting twist to information and it offers an arena for discussion and research. Introduce this activity in a simple conversational way. Let students develop the direction and if necessary support with ideas and suggestions about how it should develop.

According to research by the What's for Dinner Club, most British families live off the same food every week – an unchanging diet based on six recipes.

1 Traditional roast chicken – 30% of homes
2 Spaghetti bolognese – 27% of homes
3 Stir fry – 12% of homes
4 Sausage and mash – 12% of homes
5 Curry – 10% of homes
6 Pork chops – 7% of homes.

Interestingly, of the families taking part in the research, only two per cent reported that they cooked another dish most often. The challenge for your students is to design and plan the marketing for six currently unknown meals to guarantee their acceptance by 98% of UK families. The meals need to become the six meals that most of the population in the UK will regard as their basic and most popular meals. The meals must respectively contain:

- Insects
- Fungus
- Plankton
- Seaweed
- Nettles
- Whelks.

Canto Ostinato ad libitum

"Ipsissima verba = strictly word by word"

This activity is very different from the normal curriculum and it is very challenging. It offers a challenge that requires a high level of creativity, discipline and higher-order thinking.

Ad libitum is Latin for 'at one's pleasure' (at liberty); it is often shortened to 'ad lib' and is used as an adjective, adverb, verb or noun. As a direction in sheet music, *ad libitum* indicates that the performer or conductor can play the passage in free time rather than in strict metronomic tempo.

Normally when reading a book or a story we read in a sequential manner to understand the narrative; there is a beginning, a middle and an end. What difference would it make to the experience of reading a book if it were read ad libitum, i.e. in the same way as we read music when ad libitum directs that everything is rearrangeable? With a word processor we can move and mix words, paragraphs and titles as we feel appropriate, creating new meanings and new 'books' perhaps unintended by the original author.

Try applying this principal to an existing work of fiction. Select passages to be read several times before moving on; suggest reading slowly or quickly at different times. Some parts of the book could be read out loud, in unison, in a round, other parts sung or read quietly, in a different language or at a different pitch.

An ad libitum public reading in your local library as a part of a local literary festival would be a great focus for this activity.

Teaching tip

This may appear to be complicated. Take a little while to introduce the idea to your students and see what they make of it and how they interpret the activity. In this way, working together, there is less likelihood of anyone being confused or frustrated. It should be made clear that there is no wrong answer and that everyone has a response to this challenge that will be judged by the originality and artistic integrity of the work.

Bonus idea ★

Ask your gifted and talented students to all read copies of the same book. Ask them to see if they can recognise lines or paragraphs that have a sound rhythm. When they have finished reading the book and identified rhythm material they could sing or plain chant these sections and form a 'Reading choir'.

Nociceptors or not, it looks like pain

"I know there is no justification for causing animals pain."

Gifted and talented students usually have an interest in ethical questions and are passionate in their viewpoints. Offer them a situation to explore ethical issues which ensures them a fair hearing where the peer group they are working with acts as a critical friend during discussions.

Teaching tip

Assess your students' understanding of the research skills and issues you have presented to them by getting them to do formal presentations to you and their fellow students. By doing this you can judge their understanding of the necessary knowledge and skills whilst also enlisting your other students to be active critical friends.

Bonus idea ★

Start an ethics group! Remember you do not have to run the group. Find someone who is interested in ethical issues: a colleague, a member of the whole school team, a governor, a parent or a local professor of ethics!

In mammals, nociceptors are sensory neurons that in humans respond to potentially damaging stimuli by sending signals to the brain, allowing them to feel pain. They are found in any area of the body that can sense pain, either externally or internally, such as the skin or muscles.

Fish have been found to have nociceptors sensory receptors too, though fish are considered by some researchers to be impervious to pain because they do not have the necessary brainpower to register the effect of the nociceptors. Ask your students how they would find out whether fish feel pain without causing them pain.

- Introduce and discuss with your students the concept of ethical research.
- Remind your students of the basic rules and procedures of conducting research.
- Help your students define the focus of their research question.
- Introduce and discuss the standard research methods that researchers normally follow.

When you have covered these points ask your students to submit a research proposal that can be evaluated by their peers

Extra-terrestrial botanics

"Which do you think is preferable, classifying things using numbers and letters or using names?" "Both."

Understanding the reasoning behind classification and the possibility of creating a new form of classification exercise the areas of higher-order thinking, reasoning and logic.

The application of scientific names to plants is governed by two international codes followed throughout the world. One is the International Code of Botanical Nomenclature (ICBN). There is also the International Code of Nomenclature for Cultivated Plants. All plant names must conform to these two codes. However both of these protocols and procedures relate to the naming and classification of plants found on Earth.

What system of nomenclature would your students propose for plants found on other planets? What would they propose for example as an appropriate classification and procedure for the naming of a new plant found on Mars? What is the scientific knowledge and logic behind the system that justifies their recommendation?

When a new system of interplanetary naming and classification of plants supported by logical reasoning is agreed upon by your students they could send their considerations to The Secretary General, International Association for Plant Taxonomy (Europe) Institute of Botany in Bratislava, Slovakia.

It would be fascinating to find out what the Institute thinks of your students' ideas. Your students may define the classification of plants found in outer space and on planets as yet unknown and unnamed.

Teaching tip

This activity could be used in a science lesson as enrichment to any exploration of the systems of classification which underpin scientific work. The issues raised may not be pressing, as finding plants or life in space may be some way in the future, but the possibility is real and potentially even within the lives of your students.

Unlikely musical

"I'm good at lots of things but I don't let school know. Everyone thinks I'm good at maths but I really like writing music."

Working with others can sometimes be problematic for gifted and talented students. This may be due to the limited thinking speeds, lack of creativity, poor problem solving, and weak empathy skills of other students causing the able student to feel isolated and frustrated. This idea will help promote an understanding that different people have different skills and talents that can and should be respected and that all abilities and skills have a part to play in improving and developing the quality of all our lives.

Teaching tip

The discussion that follows could be humorous, light hearted or profound. Remember able children have a highly-developed sense of humour and enjoy complexity. For example the Einstein/Graf musical could easily be about time and space or tennis! Einstein said that if he had not been a physicist he would have probably been a musician.

Taking it further

An important part of any successful production is effective marketing. Your students could create a Twitter, Facebook or YouTube campaign to make their musical famous and a must-see. They could aim to create a buzz around the event even before they have finished it.

Ask your students to write down the names of famous people from any point in history. Have your students write 20 names onto slips of paper, mix the slips up and ask each student to choose two slips from the mixed up selection. Unlikely partnerships will be the result, perhaps a partnership such as Einstein and Steffi Graf. Next, ask students to imagine these two people combined their talents to write a musical. Students should then write their own musical based on these unlikely partnerships.

They should:

1 Write down the song list. This will bring a structure to the musical and allow them to get a sense of how long the musical will be.
2 Write the script and music. Indicating stage directions is a good idea if care is taken to avoid too much control over the movements of singers and actors. As the musical evolves, they will find useful ideas and suggestions for stage directions will be provided by the people in the production.
3 Perform to invited groups, invite every theatrical reviewer you can find to come and experience your new musical.

Super sleep

"Can I get a pillow from the sick room?"

Quality sleep and the ability or inability to relax are very important issues for the gifted and talented student who will put themselves under great pressure all the time to achieve.

Research carried out by Amy R. Wolfson and Mary A. Carskadon show that for some groups of students poor sleep quality is negatively associated with academic performance from secondary school through to the college years. It would appear that getting enough sleep is important, the question is how much is enough?

Invite your students to make themselves as comfortable as they can. Tell them they can go to sleep, daydream or meditate for however much time you have available for the session, for example 20 minutes out of a 30 minute teaching slot. You could provide a meditation commentary to help them relax or play some soothing music. Whatever you do, make sure the space you are working in is safe and not prone to sudden interruptions.

At the end of the sleeping part of the session, ask students to say their name to themselves and remind themselves where they are and what they are doing. This is important as it helps them deal with any difficulties they may have begun to address during their sleep and also helps them to simply wake up! Some students will fall into a deep sleep, others will relax and others will just wriggle about.

When everyone is awake ask the question, 'did you enjoy your sleep?' The answers will be varied and lead to a discussion about individual behaviour and circumstances that may need addressing or offer welcome tips on how to relax and enjoy quality sleep.

Teaching tip

Be prepared for this activity to take more than one session. Be patient with those students who start to have the giggles or 'nudge' others. Explain in a calm voice that 'Yes, some people will giggle and be silly. This is normal and will pass.' It is a strange thing to be asked to do in school and a lot of relaxation and bubbling anxiety can be released the first time this activity is tried out. Persevere! You may have people fall fast asleep – wake them up calmly and quietly. You may have students cry. Reassure them and make sure they have an opportunity to talk with you privately.

Bonus idea ★

Try this yourself! Find a time and a suitable place to take 10 or 20 minutes of silent time. It does not matter if you sleep, what matters is that you allow time to become calm and maintain a sense of perspective.

The interabang!?

"He's obsessed with the apostrophe. Nothing else, just the apostrophe."

Tweeting, emailing and instant messaging cause punctuation to develop beyond accepted conventions. This idea is a playful exploration of language and structure.

We are all familiar with normal punctuation symbols and their application. For most students the exclamation mark or full stop hold no fear. The use of punctuation is clear and has served writers well as it has developed and become accepted standard practice to be followed.

Ask your students which punctuation mark or symbol is their favourite or that they find indispensable.

Introduce the notion of combining punctuation marks in new ways. Explain the Interabang and its use as a nonstandard punctuation mark intended to combine the functions of the question mark and the exclamation mark.

Allowing your students the use of all keyboard symbols to create additional punctuation forms, what other punctuation combinations would prove useful in allowing greater expression through punctuation? What might the applications be for a combined full stop and a bracket .] or perhaps a double colon ::?

Wireless cars

"Since I started teaching, my car has become an office."

Gifted and talented students should be presented with challenging, complex ideas. This idea involves technology as well as social and economic issues.

Some public transport buses in South Korea are using online electric vehicle technology (OLEV) where they are charged by taking power from the road as they drive along. Although the costs of installing the necessary technology in the roads is high, there are cost savings through the reduction of heavy batteries being used to power buses. One significant benefit of the electric buses using OLEV is significantly reduced carbon emissions.

Other pilot programmes are using vehicles that are wirelessly-charged. At Utah State University, a wirelessly-charged bus has been reported to be working at a 90% efficiency rate of power transmission. There are prototype experimental cars being trialled using the wireless charging system in London.

Ask your students to consider the implication of fuel-free electric vehicles, which can be charged as they drive around cities and towns. Is there a need in the future for public transport as we know it in the form of the bus? What will happen to the economics surrounding the supply of fossil fuels for vehicles?

Teaching tip

If and when you feel that you do not have the expertise or experience to present and support a project, try advertising for an enthusiast. A note in all registers asking that anyone with a knowledge or interest in wireless-controlled cars should result in at least one enthusiastic student (or staff member) getting in contact. Ask and invite help.

Bonus idea ★

Invite your students to design and make a model of a wireless electric person transporter vehicle. What will the interior be like without a fuel tank or conventional engine? What will the exterior of the car be like without having all the features associated with the petrol/diesel engine? Discuss, draw, evaluate and make a model of the design which could become a radio-controlled model if not a wireless-charged model.

Taking stock and taking control of the gifted and talented provision

Part 9

The gifted and talented coordinator

"I love the responsibility of being in charge of the gifted and talented provision for our school; it is so rewarding."

The gifted and talented coordinator is a role which requires close attention to monitoring the effective provision made for gifted and talented students, as well as monitoring their success and progress and enabling them to develop into independent and confident learners.

The effective gifted and talented coordinator needs to:

- Identify all the able, gifted and talented students, including the underachievers and students with double exceptionality.
- Keep an up-to-date register of names and records of progress for each student.
- Act as a resourceful champion and diplomat working towards raising the achievement and securing the motivation of gifted and talented students throughout the school.
- Coordinate provision for able, gifted and talented students on the school register.
- Keep colleagues informed and provide support for their work with the gifted and talented.
- Manage a budget (if one exists).
- Develop appropriate teaching methods and effective practice in all lessons and in turn be a model of excellent classroom practice.
- Ensure good communications with the parents and carers of the students on the gifted and talented register; providing knowledge about high ability and all the possible associated challenges that students, their teachers and families may experience.

The key to success is effective and regular data management and good communications.

Creative careers

"I want to grow up and originate space graffiti."

How does a creative and highly-gifted student find a career?

For the academically-able student with a particular talent there are well-defined routes into professions and opportunities. For the student who is highly creative the world offers somewhat less in the way of open doors.

Students with a highly individual and creative view of the world face the difficulty of finding their way into areas that are difficult to access such as working artists' studios and starting up new and innovative professional activities. Even more difficult is for a young person to become, for example, resident artist on the space station. The creative, gifted and talented student can see the possibilities and connections that many of us will struggle to immediately understand or accept. These students need more than the usual understanding and patience offered to other gifted and talented students.

They should not be patronised nor should they be indulged. They should be helped in the best way you can by arranging meetings, networking opportunities and encouragement. There are many websites and other resources emerging and being developed to support the creative mind. Help your students to access these materials, enter competitions, seek scholarships and residential opportunities.

They may be clever but they are still young, often disorganised, emotionally sensitive and enjoy an intense imaginative awareness of the world, coupled with a strong sense of fantasy. They need your critical adult experience to help them grow and develop.

Teaching tip

Guided dreaming or guided imagining can help the highly-creative student visualise career potential and opportunities that relate to their personalities. The result of successful dreaming/meditation can be very relaxing and support the development of the dreamer's self-understanding. It is a good idea when suggesting to your students what they should focus on when dreaming that they involve all their senses. Imagine they can 'see' their dream, 'hear' it, imagine the 'feel' of the dream, imagine the 'smell' and 'sounds' of the dream. If you are unfamiliar with the techniques of guided dreaming ask your drama department or SENCO to help with expertise and guidance.

The joy of getting it wrong

"Sometimes getting it wrong is the right thing to do."

Aim for a balanced understanding by your students and remember that mistakes are useful learning and clarification opportunities.

It is not realistic to eliminate from the popular thinking cultural norm that mistakes are bad. It will be a slow process to establish that while mistakes are not necessarily good or bad in themselves, they are useful if you adopt a positive approach to handling them. The danger with mistakes is that they may prevent students from being willing to take opportunities to try new ideas or activities because of a sense of failure.

Mistakes should be seen as legitimate learning opportunities, which offer a chance to be directed to solutions as well as even more learning opportunities. Mistakes are simply a way of having the need for clarity and understanding addressed. The presence of lots of mistakes in a teaching and learning situation points to a need for a different approach in teaching methodology. The old adage is true, we do learn from our mistakes.

Offer your gifted and talented cohort the opportunity to complete a past exam paper in, for example, English. The one new exam regulation you introduce and require from them is that no answer they provide can in any way be seen as a right answer. This is a very funny thing to do but also very difficult as well. When the exam is finished ask students to mark each other's papers. Natural competition and delight will mean that even the most remote connection to a right answer will be pursued relentlessly. Discuss with your students whether this exercise was enjoyable or not and what could be learnt from it.

SWOTing up

"I like the bad news first, it helps concentrate the mind."

A SWOT analysis looks at: strengths, weaknesses, opportunities and threats. Put one together to assess the gifted and talented provision in your school.

Begin by noting down under the heading **Strengths** what you believe you and your school do well. Do you, for instance, have a good procedure for identifying gifted and talented students? How do those involved in the care and nurture of your gifted and talented students see your strengths? Ask students, parents, colleagues, non-teaching staff, governors and other colleagues who visit the school on an occasional basis about their views.

Under **Weaknesses** take a hard and honest look at what could be improved. Do you have good record keeping? Is enrichment in the classroom an accepted part of classroom activity?

When looking at **Opportunities** ask a simple question, what opportunities are available that you can utilise to enrich the educational experience of your students? How can you turn strengths into opportunities?

Threats can often be the most interesting section of a SWOT analysis. What could damage the progress you have already made and intend to make in the near future? Will the time resources and financial resources available to you be reduced in the future? Are you in danger of becoming a lone voice for the gifted and talented? Should you work more with other gifted and talented teachers from other schools?

Good role models

"She was a real challenge at school and now she owns six florist shops."

The best role model a gifted and talented student can have is you.

Be an example of enthusiasm for learning, curiosity and openness to new ideas, flexibility and spontaneity. You can be you.

The danger in supplying examples of role models and examples of success is that a student will see these examples as the way to be and seek to emulate others' performances. A context and narrative associated with any role models you may introduce to the creative gifted and talented child should always emphasise the unique journey, obstacles and hurdles overcome, determination to succeed and an absolute belief in the individual need to do and achieve what they did. Everyone has his or her own story.

Keeping the above proviso in mind, in addition to being an example to your students, you can provide examples of successful creative thinkers, artists, entrepreneurs, inventors, musicians and architects. People with vision have many things in common.

As an exercise over time you could invite your creative gifted students to research people who have achieved alternative success in society and innovated modern life with systems, products or thinking. We all depend upon the development and success of the creative person, trained to think, and given the opportunity to make the future.

Delivering professional development to colleagues

"Nurturing higher achievement amongst students is often about realising the true enthusiasms of colleagues within the school setting."

As often as possible, work with other colleagues to share ideas and develop a greater understanding of the gifted and talented agenda.

There are two key aspects which make providing professional development with regard to the gifted and talented worthwhile:

- The first is it increases the whole school support and understanding of the special needs of the gifted and talented.
- The second benefit is that it increases the chance that other colleagues will wish to work with you on developing work and activities that focus on both differentiation and enrichment/extension.

When you are able to, feed ideas and news about gifted and talented issues into staff meetings. Develop colleagues' understanding of gifted and talented issues through a staffroom noticeboard which you keep fresh and up-to-date. Be ruthless about carrying the flag for the gifted and talented.

After you have provided a training event for teachers either from your school or partner schools it is a very effective training tool to supply a learning summary of the event either as a hard copy or as an email. Always tell people three times to make sure an idea sticks. In the case of INSET the first time is when they are told about the training, the second time is the training itself and the third telling is your follow-up summary. Make learning easy for everyone.

Teaching tip

Never moan about having to go to meetings! Meetings are a great way of keeping in touch with what is happening in your school. Meetings are also about finding out what other people are trying to achieve, what resources they have and what plans they are developing for the school, school trips, speakers and so forth. All information is useful for you to help people achieve their goals while helping you achieve yours. Gather Intelligence. Information is always useful.

Socialising experiences

"Yeah, it's the same with me at my school. I'm the only one interested in subatomic particles."

Congregating gifted and talented students together is necessary for their social development.

Whatever your feelings or your school's decisions about how children should be organised, whether in groupings, streaming, banding or setting, there is a good argument for bringing gifted minds together. Gifted and talented students together can improve individual motivation, challenge assumptions and raise individual and group standards of achievement and learning.

One surprising outcome from gifted and talented students working together on appropriate challenges is an increased commitment to individual learning and achievement. Any student, particularly the able, gifted and talented student, will aspire to achieve what he or she regards as their peer group standard.

Gifted and talented students working together have an opportunity to challenge ideas, develop friendships, share interests and experience different enthusiasms as experienced by the other students they work with.

For some students, continually working at levels and with fellow students who are not as intellectually able can lead to a destructive attitude being developed and this attitude will be accompanied with a boredom and sense of frustration, neither of which are conducive to learning.

Surviving as a gifted and talented coordinator

"Come back!" the Caterpillar called after her. "I've something important to say." This sounded promising, certainly. Alice turned and came back again. "Keep your temper," said the Caterpillar."
Lewis Carroll, *Alice's Adventures in Wonderland.*

Managing the pressure of having responsibility for the gifted and talented students in your school should not be left to luck.

The pressures of being the person with responsibility for gifted and talented students in your school can be reduced by good management practice. Do not try to be a 'do it all' leader.

1 Make sure that all teachers and assistants have clear information about how to work with the gifted and talented.
2 Make material you think will work to enrich and extend particular subject areas available to subject specialists and departments.
3 Keep your colleagues up-to-date with gifted and talented issues through a noticeboard display or the school staff intranet.
4 Find a gifted and talented work partner who is willing to help you with activities and support your gifted and talented students. It does not matter how new to the profession or how experienced the colleague is, some people just love working with clever students.
5 Check that your school policy and strategy for identification of gifted and talented students are crystal clear for all parents to see and understand.

Teaching tip

Keep a diary of how you feel and your sense of achievement for a week or two and then find a moment to read through the records you have made to see if any patterns emerge about when projects, activities and ideas work well and when perhaps they are not so successful. Can you identify issues you need to address?

Perfect provision

"It's all about opening doors so eager minds can learn and explore, and not worrying about the fact that your students are likely to be cleverer than you. I learn a lot from my students."

The role of the gifted and talented coordinator is complex but rewarding. This idea provides a student feedback approach to improving your provision.

The key to success as coordinator is to develop clear working structures for your students and an understanding that they need a teacher and co-learner who will respect them and act as their champion. However, how do your students perceive what they want and what do they expect in the way of provision?

Construct a questionnaire for your gifted and talented students to complete. It should include questions concerning:

- Provision for them in the classroom.
- The setting and marking of homework.
- Is the provision of enrichment and extension work sufficiently personalised for them?
- Examples of what they consider good teaching (anonymous!).
- Examples of bad teaching (anonymous!).
- Is their work and progress clearly monitored and are they a part of this?
- Do they play any part in planning their enriched curriculum?
- Do they think all the able, gifted and talented students in the school have been identified?
- Is there enough pastoral support for them?
- What would they see as 'perfect provision for them' and how can the school improve what is done for them, their families and carers.

Collect the returns, analyse the content and produce an action plan for improving your school's provision.

Bonus idea ★

Ask your students to consider what would go into a student 'Off sick' learning pack. Occasionally students are poorly and need time off school. As they recover their physical health they will also recover their need for intellectual stimulation. What would go into a 'Getting Better Learner Pack'? Task your students with producing such a pack which could then be prepared in advance saving time when 'work for home' needs to be produced.

If you were doing it all again

"I always start at the back of a book."

Gifted and talented students can be demanding, they can also be the most rewarding students you will ever work with.

The reward of working with the gifted and talented student is a double reward. As a teacher you have the joy of working with and guiding a growing intelligence that will reveal new insights into your understanding of the universe while also allowing you an opportunity to share in the invention of the future.

Whether you are experienced or new to working with the gifted and talented, ask yourself what you would do if you were to do it all again. Whatever you are doing throughout your career and life, it is a good rule to occasionally reflect on what you are doing, how you are doing it and what that suggests that you should be doing in the future. This does not have to be done alone, it can usefully be done by those you work with.

If I were doing it all again, would I do it at all? Teaching the gifted and talented is not something everyone enjoys. If this is your answer then be honest and seek a new direction. This is not, as it may seem, a negative suggestion, it is a positive one.

If I were doing it all again, I would relax and enjoy it more; I would offer greater challenges; I wouldn't worry about not understanding the advanced work of my students. If this is how you feel then the future for you and the gifted and talented looks good. You have the experience and ability to teach a challenging group and they have an overpowering need to know everything; a perfect partnership, especially if you share that need as well.

Teaching tip

As a teacher of the able student you are given the opportunity to have glimpses of exciting thinking, new thoughts, fresh understanding of familiar ideas, see the future and see the past through excited and stimulating intellects. Truly share the learning and enjoy the fact that you can fly high as well as your students.

Enrichment ideas 5

Part 10

The three wise women

"I'm lucky; we tend to attract the brightest students to R.E."

The question of gender and influence can be legitimately discussed as a part of emotional development, historic speculation, and citizenship.

According to the Gospel of Matthew, the Magi were the first religious figures to worship Jesus. The Bible does not say there were only three wise men. There could have been many more. We assume that there were three wise men, Caspar, Melchior, and Balthasar, because of the three gifts they brought: gold, frankincense and myrrh (Matthew 2:11).

A Church of England committee revising the latest Church of England prayer book said the term Magi was a transliteration of the name used by officials at the Persian court, and that they could well have been women.

Welcome a discussion with your students about this matter. If, from the beginning, the reported event of the Magi visiting Jesus had mentioned three wise women, would the account have had a different effect on the world? What changes can they imagine? How would our lives be lived today? How would this interpretation have changed history?

- What names would the three wise women have had?
- How would they have dressed and appeared?
- What gifts would the three wise women have brought for the baby?

Teaching tip

Support this discussion if necessary by introducing some examples of gender swaps. Imagine if the first human being on the Moon was female and not male. Do your students feel that male to female swaps have the same consequences as female to male swaps?

Taking it further

Ask your students to consider the gender ratio within their school. A staffing profile would be fascinating to discuss. What effect do your students think would occur if the ratios of male/female staff were reversed? Even more interestingly would be to ask your students to recall the gender mix in their primary school experience. What observations are made about who does what in their school?

Dictionary of the unacceptable

"I sometimes used to wonder who got more embarrassed when we had the relationships talk, me or the students."

Gifted and talented students really enjoy the hair-raising avenues and byways of thinking and going places few others would think of going. This idea will go anywhere and will be different each time.

By 1850, the French writer Gustave Flaubert had largely completed his *Dictionary of Accepted Ideas*. In the dictionary, words and phrases are defined in such ways as to give both a humourous, sometimes cynical and often satirical meaning. The dictionary, alongside Flaubert's last novel, *Bouvard and Pecuchet* is extremely funny and informative. The dictionary provokes thinking and challenges lazy assumptions about what things mean or do not mean.

This idea is challenging. Ask your students as a group to produce a dictionary of things they find it hard to talk about, from A to Z containing 24 entries under each letter of the alphabet. They will have to work very hard to complete the task but it will be worth it, as it will explore the challenges and difficulties we have as a society. In completing and researching the dictionary a lot of discussion will occur, as well as a lot of analysis, debate and thoughtfulness.

When the dictionary is complete it will be a stunning resource for discussions all about the fears, anxieties and needs of our society.

Catalytic clothing

"It's good to be able to work in my own way and not having someone telling me what to do all the time."

This idea is designed to stimulate creativity. It provides an opportunity to think, talk and make clothing with a new environmental perspective.

Clothing is, generally speaking, divided into three categories: functional, fashionable, or a hybrid of functional and fashionable. This activity invites your students to think about design and make new clothing that not only functions as clothes should, but also contributes to improving the environment too.

Catalytic clothing is a concept that looks at how clothing and textiles can be used as a catalytic surface to purify air or any other positive function.

Employing existing technology in a new way, students could consider future clothing and textile demands with regard to climate change, health issues, improving education or any other major issue facing our species. For example, clothing that neutralises the effects of body odour on crowded transport may be useful. The side effects of neutralising pheromones may not always be welcome as they are used to seek out compatible companionship through smell attraction. What could be the consequences of neutralising pheromones?

When your students have discussed the issues involved (materials, technology, style and side effects) they can then design and make a model of their idea. The next stage is to assess the problems that they have encountered and solve any issues that have arisen before moving on to making a full wearable garment. The finished pieces can be showcased at a school fashion show.

Teaching tip

Make sure everyone taking part in this activity is given health and safety training on any machinery or tools they may use. This is very important, some gifted and talented students may forget the unforgiving nature of technology and become lost in the rush to manufacture and fabricate at the price of safe working practices.

Style makes the difference

"I've never known anyone borrow so many plates."

Gifted and talented students are capable of making great commitment to their work whether they choose to be a clinical psychologist, surgeon or researcher engineer. This idea presents an opportunity to consider what is important enough to them to give so much commitment. This idea is also about developing opportunities.

If you are a business or economics teacher this will be familiar ground. If you are unfamiliar with business planning then seek advice from a suitable colleague. You could, as an alternative approach, invite a bank representative business advisor to come and advise your group.

Ask your students to identify the major styles of each decade of the last 100 years. What do the styles from each decade tell your students about the political ideologies of that particular decade? Are there any patterns between, for example, styles in clothing and political activity? Can they predict from their research what styles to expect in the near future and what this will be accompanied by in respect of political activity?

Food stylists cook, source and buy ingredients, find props, do a lot of washing up and anything else that makes sure food is beautifully presented and arranged for the perfect photograph or film. In addition, they normally get up at about 6.30am ready for a day that could end at 6.28am the following day.

Ask your students if they can think of any opportunities to style other areas of consumption such as their school, themselves, their teachers, houses or cars for sale, healthy attitudes, charities, in fact anything! The task involves looking at every aspect of a person, service or product and maximising its attractiveness to other people, consumers or supporters.

When they have considered and chosen their particular interest they should be supported in creating a business plan to make the opportunity they have envisioned a reality.

The real challenge is getting a feature article published all about your particular stylist endeavour.

How far can you throw an idea?

"To let everyone know something quickly I usually tell one or two people 'in confidence' and word generally gets round instantly."

This idea aims to encourage your students to consider and then develop the next great idea in communications technology and follow in the footsteps of Tim Berners-Lee, inventor of the Internet. Future new communication technologies will require constant innovation in communications. Presented with this problem your students will arrive at a solution and be a part of the new innovations. The solution they arrive at may be the next step.

In his elegant book *Mathematics: a very short introduction,* Timothy Gowers discusses how the forces of science and mathematics working together maximise the distance a stone can be skimmed across water. If we seek to maximise our achievement of communicating an idea to as many people as possible in the shortest time we could consider making the same combination of science and mathematics as well.

Good communicators are efficient. The bee, upon returning to a hive can communicate through a series of dancing movements, to all the bees in the hive in an incredibly short time.

Email can be sent to many people in a very small amount of time. In order to receive the information they need to read their emails (and be familiar with the language you have written your communication in). Telephones, texts, radio and TV broadcasts, newspapers and posters all communicate at different rates.

Ask your students to consider and model the most effective way of communicating a message to every person in a large city (or country if they are feeling courageous) in the shortest amount of time and without the message being changed in anyway. What do they think are the strengths and weaknesses of different types of communication?

> **Teaching tip**
>
> This idea is realised and accelerated if you or your students have a working understanding of mathematical modelling. If you don't, invite someone you know who understands mathematical modelling to visit and communicate this understanding to others.

You are what you read

"It must be true; I read it on the Internet."

This idea is designed to support the gifted and talented student in becoming a critical reader.

A way of talking about believing what you read is to try different ways of looking at news broadcasts, interviews and film reportage from the perspective of body language. Even the best presenters leak their true feelings to the camera.

With the printed word it is more difficult. Persuasive words are very powerful in getting us to agree with the views of others.

Suggest that your students try a few techniques to evaluate the news and features they may read in newspapers, magazines or on the Internet. Invite them to consider what they are really being told.

Suggest the following activities to your students.

- Read similar articles from different sources out loud to spot the editing and differences in style.
- Read a news item from the Internet as a printed hard copy in an unusual setting, this detaches the information from the surrounding context.
- Play charades and express the news article or feature as a charade performance. This will force a focus on the absolute essentials of the article.

When students have had the experience of viewing news from a variety of perspectives, what are their thoughts? Have a discussion. Part of the discussion could be: is news being passed on or is propaganda and opinion being passed off as news?

Sneaky sensory inactivation

"I dropped all my grades by two levels (except maths) and then I had more friends. It was easy to pull the marks back for assessments and exams."

While a great deal of thought is given to how we attract interest from other members of our species, little is discussed about how we avoid their interest. This idea offers an opportunity to increase your students, understanding of anthropological issues and offer a cathartic experience for your students who often have to manage unwanted attentions from bullies and others who do not respect them as people.

It is generally accepted that chemical inking by sea hares (*Aplysia*), cuttlefish, squid and octopuses is used as a form of defence allowing them to escape predators. It is not clear exactly how inking actually works, whether for example, the ink acts on the predator's systems directly or acts by producing visual confusion. There is evidence that an animal that uses chemicals to defend itself not only avoids being eaten but can additionally avoid a prospective predator by detecting its chemical signature which will in turn trigger evasive activity.

The important point is that by using chemicals sea hares, cuttlefish, squid, octopuses, the parrot fish and baby lizards can defend themselves by essentially doing nothing except confusing the enemy in a non-destructive way.

Read or adapt the above information for your students and ask them to discuss and consider the question: how can the use of chemicals and the technique described above be adapted to protect human beings from human beings?

> **Teaching tip**
>
> Students are very highly tuned to survival techniques, especially the able student. Through this idea you can gain a very clear insight into the issues that impact on the well-being of your group. Great emotional distress can involve perfectionism, anxieties and pathological behaviour which can all be big parts of some students' lives. Offer an opportunity to talk openly about these important matters through the sea hare!

What does food dream about?

"I had a dream last night that I was a cake."

This type of idea can be used to indirectly discuss matters of identity; a difficult question for the emotionally intelligent and sensitive student.

We often anthropomorphise animals, we can imagine them living lives in the world, with relationships mirroring human beings. We imagine animals talking, singing, dancing, going on adventures and dreaming, but what about food?

Ask your students to think about anthropomorphosis and how it influences how we see and think about the world. Then introduce into the discussion if animals dream and what they dream about, perhaps choose one or two animals to consider. Moving onto what food dreams about will by this time appear a perfectly normal question of the more surreal kind and a jolly discussion should follow. This activity will inform an understanding of our relationships both metaphysical and physical concerning animals. It will also be a useful introduction into the area of dream psychology and therapy work. Does a fish pie dream about mathematics? (Fish pi).

In lucid dreams it is claimed that the dreamer can direct his or her dreams. Ask your students to consider who they are by day and who they are by dream. What would they choose to dream about and why?

Plumbing and philosophy

"My Dad's a bricklayer and more of an art critic than a philosopher."

The career paths and destinations of able, gifted and talented students are not always predictable. This activity supports the student in understanding the sociological and political-economic features influencing the world of employment.

Start the discussion by asking what your students aspire to do with their lives. Do they have specific jobs or careers in mind? Why do they choose what they have chosen? The conversation can then follow on from you asking the question: is there a hierarchy of occupations? What is it? What does any hierarchy tell us about the society we live in?

Further discussion can involve questions such as: is the hierarchy list of occupations good or bad for society? Is there a list of careers which are good for the individual involved but bad for society? Should all jobs have a 'good for society' element within them to pay back for the education a person received up to university?

When the discussion has established a hierarchy of careers and opportunities, two questions could then be asked.

1 How does the present education system meet the development of the careers that are considered important?
2 How should an education system be designed to meet the need for suitable people to be employed in the most prestigious and socially rewarding careers?

Teaching tip

As a teacher and a significant person in influencing students' views, one should always be careful about expressing personal views. Break the rule with this one, bearing in mind you have more experience of work, careers and actually living with career choices than your students. Join in the discussion!

Taking it further

Get your students to produce a list of what they regard as the top ten jobs it is possible to have in this decade. The discussion point would be which of these jobs will still be needed in the next decade? Can your students also predict the jobs that will appear in the near future that do not exist today? What basic education do your students consider necessary to enable people to be ready to take up the new professions/ jobs or possible life-time of non-employment?

Safe havens

"Give me your tired, your poor, Your huddled masses yearning to breathe free; The wretched refuse of your teeming shore, Send these, the homeless, Tempest-tossed to me, I lift my lamp beside the golden door!"
Emma Lazarus, Inscription on the Statue of Liberty

This idea is designed to create an informed view amongst your students of the serious issues of the plight of some 56 million people in the world suffering now, of whom nearly half are their age. It will also develop and support the development of higher-order thinking skills in the humanities, social sciences, economics, media studies and management studies. It is a long detailed idea that could be set as an extended research topic that covers a series of lessons.

Teaching tip

You would be wise to look at the resources available from the UNHCR who produce a monthly update on the latest news, events and publications from the UK and around the world. In addition UNHCR publish on a wide range of issues, including The Global Appeal and Global Report. It would also be a good idea to see what helpful resources the geographers in the humanities department could provide for you to use: maps, pictures and reference material for example. The historians in the same department could help by providing or suggesting materials concerned with the rise of cities and city-states. UNHCR: http://www.unhcr.org.uk/

The surface area of our world is approximately 197 million square miles, which supports a population of approximately 6.9 billion people. The greater mass of people live in highly-concentrated areas such as cities, that are nearly always near to a coastline. Probably the most densely-populated city in the world is Shanghai with a population of 17,836,133.

Ask your students to consider the following figures from the United Nations High Commissioner for Refugees (UNHCR):

- There are estimated to be 12 million stateless people in dozens of countries around the world.
- The estimated figures for refugees in the world is 15.4 million people.
- The estimated number of displaced people, forcibly uprooted from their homelands within their own country is approximately 28.8 million.
- 46% of refugees are aged under 18 years old.
- The aggregated figure, world wide, of people without basic security is 56.2 million.

Invite your students to consider the establishment of new cities supported by the nations of the Earth that would ensure security and decent lives for the 56.2 million people without a safe place to live. Just 14 new cities the size Shanghai would be sufficient to accommodate every refugee and stateless person. Ask them to consider:

- Where would the cities be placed?
- What would they be called?
- How could they be funded?
- Who would administer them?
- What technology would be needed to make this concept viable (given that many remote places where new cities could be built will probably experience extremes of weather conditions)?
- What political and management institutions would the new cities need?
- What would be the nature of the governance? For example 'city states' or free-trade areas within the countries they are located?
- Who would provide defence and health services for the new cities?
- Is the formation of 'cities' preferable to other types of communities being established?

One critical point of discussion will be the environmental issues concerning 'pristine' areas of the world and their use. Possible locations for the cities could be:

- Antarctica
- Sahara Desert
- Northern Siberia
- Greenland
- West Australia Desert
- Northwest Canada.

When your students have finished their discussions, decided on locations and answered all the questions, ask them to produce a world map showing the new cities they propose with an accompanying report to explain the basis of their decisions, the logic or romance which inspired the names of the new cities and any other information they decided the reader should know.